WHAT'S GOOD

and good for you?

The answer is eggs.

Eggs are the protein-perfect food with no waste. Ounce for ounce, they're the best food buy available. From soup to soufflé, from afternoon snack to hearty main dish, eggs are the one food that can pep up your meals and put pep back into your budget.

If your family is getting tired of the same old thing, do what the smart cooks do——start cooking with eggs.

THE FABULOUS EGG COOKBOOK

JEFFREY FEINMAN

Contents

Contents

Chapter I

WHAT DO YOU KNOW ABOUT EGGS?

WHERE IN THE WORLD the eggs of the uncomplaining hen were first used for food is open to debate. Both India and China boast ancient records telling of the taming and breeding of various jungle fowl which finally gave us chickens as we know them today.

As early as 1500 B. C. the Chinese bred chickens for both sport and food. Cockfighting, a cruel sport, was a great pastime in ancient China. Prize-bred roosters were thrown into stone-lined pits to fight to the death. This sport, fortunately, has been outlawed in many countries of the world.

While the roosters of this tamed breed of jungle bird were off to the pits ripping each other to shreds, the hens were kept captive in cages to lay eggs and produce more roosters. Somewhere along the line, an ancient, wise Chinese stole some of the eggs and ate them; he found them to be a delicious food.

If a hen were left to her own devices, she would probably lay only one batch of eggs in the spring of the year. She would patiently sit on these eggs, keeping them warm until the fertile eggs produced chicks. Then, she would carefully feed the baby chicks until they were ready to fend for themselves. After this, she would lay no more eggs until the following spring; she would spend the remainder of the year socializing and clucking around the farm yard.

Normally, a hen will produce only one egg per day. The ever-vigilant farmer promptly takes this single egg from the hen and ships it to market. The more hens a farmer has, the more eggs he can get every day from their nests.

The hen is trying to accumulate a dozen or so eggs so that sitting on them to keep them warm will be worthwhile. When her egg disappears day in and day out, the little hen just keeps on replacing it with another. She has hope eternal welling up in her tender breast.

Many years ago, when the poultry and egg industry was not as mechanized as today, a good hen was expected to produce about six dozen eggs per year. Today we trick hens with lights that resemble sunlight and go on and off automatically; creating false mornings and very short nights. The hen will

7

lay an egg for a false dawn as well as a real one. Thus, egg production has been stepped up tremendously.

The amazing thing is that this forced egg production does not subtract one iota from the complete and wonderful food value contained in a single egg.

Eggs are a tremendously nutritious food. For ages, eggs have been included in the diets of the young, the healthy, the oldsters and in many therapeutic diets. Good nutrition is the reason.

Eggs are high in protein—a complete protein at that; eggs furnish all the amino acids for building and maintaining body tissues. Eggs contain vitamin A, vitamin B, thiamin (B_1), riboflavin (B_2), niacin and vitamin D. These are all necessary for good health and good growth. Eggs also contain minerals, iron and phosphorous, which are necessary for maintaining pep and vitality.

When it comes to a real food bargain, eggs win the prize. Ounce for ounce, the cheapest cut of meat at your butcher's will probably cost you about 50% more than eggs. When you consider that eggs are protein perfect with no waste, this is a great savings. One dozen two-ounce eggs weighs 1½ pounds; compare their price with 1½ pounds of meat to prove their economy to yourself.

Whether an egg is large or small it contains the same nutrients. One just has to use more of the smaller eggs to get sufficient amounts of protein, vitamins and minerals and to satisfy a hungry family.

The size of eggs is very accurately determined by their weight per dozen. This weight standard is set by the United States Department of Agriculture, and unless the egg carton bears this seal you are at the mercy of the packer or farmer. Whether the egg carton is marked "Extra Large," "Large," "Medium" or "Small" has absolutely no bearing on how the egg will taste or look after it is cooked.

Egg quality and appearance after cooking is graded as follows: AA, A, B or C. This grade is indicated on the shield of the United States Department of Agriculture which is printed on the carton itself or on the sealing tape which closes the carton. This is your most reliable buying guide when purchasing eggs.

The privilege of using the USDA shield is granted to the wholesaler or distributor of eggs only after he has been inspected and trained by a Federal-State Grader of Eggs. Wholesalers and egg distributors are thereafter inspected frequently to see that they conform to the quality standards.

Egg grades AA, A, B and C have nothing whatsoever to do with size. These gradations only determine how the egg will look when broken open and gently placed on a perfectly flat dish.

Grade AA eggs are the fancy variety. They are uniformly sized and have as near perfectly formed shells as possible. When opened, an AA egg will cover a small area. The white will be thick and stand high. The yolk is firm and high. Naturally, grade AA eggs are good for all purposes; however, they are best for frying or poaching, where their appearance has to be most appetizing and eye catching.

Grade A eggs will cover a moderate area when opened on a flat plate. Their white portion will be reasonably thick and the yolk will stand fairly high. These too can be used where serving appearance is important.

Grade B eggs will cover a wide area when opened and will have a small amount of thick white and a greater amount of thin white. The yolk is somewhat flattened and enlarged.

Grade C eggs will cover a very wide area when opened. There will be little or no thick white surrounding the yolk. The yolk itself will be flat and greatly enlarged. Both grade B and C eggs are ideal for general purposes such as sauces or cakes.

The freshness of eggs is another whole field of discussion. With today's fast transportation and modern efficient refrigeration, you do not have too much worry about eggs not being fresh or palatable.

The flavor of eggs, too, is assured the consumer; poultry farmers found out a long time ago that if their hens are fed a correctly balanced diet, their eggs will be well-flavored and their egg production high. Poor diet and food for hens result in mal-shaped eggs and low output. Eggs not properly shaped with thin, uneven shells are just not saleable by today's standards.

All of the eggs in your food market bearing the USDA seal have been inspected for size and shell appearance before they are candled. If the shells are dark spotted or uneven, the eggs are immediately rejected.

The color of the shell of the egg has absolutely no bearing on quality or freshness. Eggs may vary from pure white to a deep brown. This color is a characteristic of the breed of the chicken laying the egg. Whether the egg is white, light tan or a warm brown makes no difference in the nutritive value, flavor or cooking results. Shell color rarely enters into the grading of an egg. Easter time may be the exception to this; then there is a

9

demand for snow white eggs because they take the dyes a little better and the colors come out a little clearer.

Egg candling is a foolproof method of judging the freshness and thereby the grade of the egg. Candling is done by placing the egg directly in front of a measured light beam. Candling shows up the air space which is formed between the inner and the outer shell membranes on the large end of the egg. Candling also shows up the position of the yolk.

The amount of air space in an egg increases by evaporation as the egg grows older. If a farmer is careless and delays getting his eggs from nest to distribution center, this air space increases hour by hour. If the air space is greater than ⅜ of an inch in depth, the farmer's eggs are judged unacceptable. Thus it is easy to see why eggs are rushed from farm to distribution center and then on to the final consumer. Delay without proper refrigeration and humidity control reduces the egg's freshness and the ultimate price the farmer receives.

Eggs kept in a cool temperature with accurately controlled humidity will keep their freshness for months. Cold storage of eggs is a very exact science.

During late summer and fall, egg production is usually very high; as winter approaches, egg production falls off somewhat. If it were not for today's combined miracle workers of controlled temperature and humidity, we would have a feast and famine type of egg supply. Thanks to scientific cold storage, we are assured of fresh, palatable eggs day in and day out.

The versatile egg is indeed important in our daily diet and in good cooking. Eggs are universally used to leaven pastry and cakes; eggs are used to add color and flavor to dishes. Eggs are used to make a tasty coating for breaded fish and meat; eggs can be used as a garnish on casseroles and on salads. They are the stable element in good salad dressing; eggs are present in delicious candies. Indeed, eggs are one of the most universal, tasty foods we are privileged to enjoy.

Chapter II

THE CARE AND HANDLING OF EGGS

HOW TO STORE EGGS: Since evaporation effects the freshness, flavor and behavior of an egg, correct storage is of prime importance. Eggs, whether cooked or raw, should always be stored in the refrigerator.

Most home refrigerators extract a certain amount of moisture from the foods stored in them. I find that if you keep eggs in an air-tight plastic container, their flavor and freshness can be retained for a much longer period of time. However, if your family uses eggs in great quantity and the turnover is fast, the eggs can be stored in the cardboard containers in which they were purchased.

Never store eggs next to highly flavored foods such as fish or onions. Due to the porous nature of their shells, the eggs will absorb these flavors, and who could get enthusiastic about a fish or onion flavored egg, especially in the morning?

Eggs should always be stored with the large end up. This will suspend the yolk properly within the white of the egg.

Never wash eggs before storing them in the refrigerator. Nature has provided an invisible, protective coating over the outside of the shell which acts as a bacteria barrier. If you wash eggs you remove this barrier, leaving the egg wide open for the invasion of bacteria which will lead to spoilage.

If possible, eggs should always be allowed to warm up to room temperature before using. This usually takes about ½ hour. Having the eggs warmed slightly and not ice cold has many advantages. It prevents breakage of the shell if you are boiling them; it also makes the whites easier to whip if you are using them in a soufflé or cake. You will find too that the yolks stand up nice and high if you fry eggs that are at room temperature.

HOW TO BOIL: This sounds pretty basic, but the truth is that an egg should never be boiled, just simmered until it is done. Boiling eggs at constant high temperature can turn a delicious egg dish into something tough, strongly flavored and totally unpalatable. Whether you are soft cooking or hard cooking eggs, the water should never be at a bubbling boil; it should be just barely simmering. Eggs coagulate when a temperature of 149° F. to 158° F. is reached. Since water boils at 212° F. you can see that egg cooking temperatures are considerably below that.

Eggs should be boiled in either a glass, enamel or stainless steel pan. Do not use aluminum for boiling eggs as they will turn the pan a nice shade of dark gray or black.

Remove only the number of eggs you are going to use from the refrigerator and allow them to warm to room temperature. Do not take out the whole carton of eggs; keep the eggs you are not using under constant refrigeration.

Whether you are going to soft cook, coddle or hard cook eggs, it is advisable to make a tiny hole in the large end of the egg. This can be done with a very sharp pin or needle. Every egg has a natural air pocket in the large end. When this air is exposed to heat and starts to expand, there is no place for it to go and the shell will pop. Providing an escape hatch for this air will prevent shell breakage during cooking.

There is a little inexpensive gadget on the market which is shaped like an egg cup with a sharp pin protruding from the bottom of the bowl. This is a pretty foolproof method of piercing egg shells and you might want to invest in one.

Soft-cooked eggs can be made by either of two methods: the cold-water method or the hot-water method.

In the cold-water method, place the eggs in a suitable pan with enough cold water so that the eggs are covered by about ½ inch of water. Place on the burner and the second the water reaches a boil, remove the pan from the heat. Cover and set aside for 2 to 4 minutes, depending upon your family's tastes. Then place the eggs under cold running water for a second or so to halt the cooking action.

In the hot-water method, bring enough water to cover the eggs to a rolling boil, and then gently place the eggs in the boiling water with a spoon. Remove from the heat, cover and let stand 6 to 8 minutes, depending again on your family's tastes. Place the eggs under cold running water for a second or so to stop the cooking action.

Should you have to keep the eggs warm for stragglers to the table, you can put them back into hot tap water after the cold water plunging. There will be no change in the egg whatever if it is kept warm in this manner.

If you ever soft cook too many eggs, the extras can be refrigerated until the next day. When you want to use them the following day, place them in hot tap water for about 15 minutes or until they are warmed to proper eating temperature. Change the warm tap water two or three times during this

12

warm-up period, because it does cool off considerably after the addition of the refrigerated eggs. This method of keeping eggs hot is used in many hospital kitchens where the demand for soft-cooked eggs would be impossible to fill in a short space of time.

Hard-cooked eggs can also be cooked by the cold-water method and the hot-water method.

For the cold-water method of hard-cooking eggs, place the eggs in a suitable pan with cold water to cover about ½ inch over the tops. Place on the burner and cook until the water reaches the boiling point. Turn off the heat and cover. Let stand for 15 minutes and then cool quickly under cold running water.

For the hot-water method of hard-cooking eggs, place enough water in a suitable saucepan to cover the eggs ½ inch over their tops. Bring the water to a rolling boil and then add the eggs by gently placing them in the water with a spoon. Turn the heat back to just below simmering, cover and cook for 20 minutes. Place the eggs under cold running water immediately.

Immediate cooling of hard-cooked eggs makes their shells easier to remove. After the eggs have been thoroughly chilled, tap them against a hard surface and crack the shell in many places; then roll the egg between your hands to further crack the shell. Peeling off the shell is easier if done under cold running water; this also prevents tiny bits of shell from clinging to the egg and getting into the dish you are preparing.

Never hard cook an egg that is less than two days old. A freshly laid egg is almost impossible to peel after being hard cooked.

Dark egg yolks in hard-cooked eggs are caused by a number of factors. You can avoid them by following these rules: First, the eggs must be fresh, but not freshly laid. Secondly, the eggs must be cooked at low temperatures. Lastly, the eggs must be chilled immediately after cooking and then kept chilled until they are used.

An off-center yolk in a hard-cooked egg is often due to the fact that the egg might not have been really fresh. If you doubt the freshness of eggs for hard cooking, turn them with a spoon several times during the cooking and this will evenly coagulate the white and help center the yolk.

If you ever doubt the freshness of eggs you have purchased, shake them next to your ear. If they make a sloshing, gurgling sound, take them back to the grocer—he shouldn't have sold them to you in the first place.

13

How to separate eggs: Eggs which are ice cold separate much more easily than eggs which are at room temperature. However, egg whites which are at room temperature whip more easily and give a greater volume of whipped white. Therefore, separate the eggs as they come out of the refrigerator and then allow them to warm up to room temperature in covered separate dishes.

If you have trouble separating eggs by the shell to shell method, try this trick. Using a sharp paring knife, make a ⅛ inch hole in the small end of the egg and allow the white to drain out slowly.

If your recipe calls for both the whites and the yolks, break the drained shell and put the yolk in a separate bowl. If your recipe calls for just egg whites, use the draining method and seal up the hole with transparent tape. Store the egg, large end down sealed hole up, in its container until you need the yolks. Be sure to mark the carton or the eggs with crayon or pencil, for you can have an early morning family holocaust if someone grabs one of these "half" eggs by mistake.

There is another little trick to separating eggs. The yolk is always located near the large end of the egg. After breaking the shell against the side of the bowl, if you hold the large end to receive the yolk first, the white will slip out of the small end easily. After the initial portion of the white has slipped away, it is easier to transfer the yolk into the small end of the shell.

Storing separated eggs: If you have a recipe that calls for just egg yolks, the remaining whites can be stored in the refrigerator in an air-tight jar up to a week.

The storage of yolks is a little more difficult. The yolks, too, should be put into an air-tight jar and covered with a few spoonfuls of boiled water which has been cooled to room temperature. Yolks can be stored in this manner for two or three days. Remember, yolks alone can be used with a little milk for breading or scrambling.

Egg yolks can also be stored by dropping them into salted, boiling water one by one after separation. Then turn the heat back to very low simmer and cook them until they are firm and hard cooked. The yolks can then be removed from the water with a slotted spoon, drained and used as a delicious garnish on salads or over the top of a casserole.

How to make egg whites really stand up: Nothing is more disheartening to a cook than to have a batch of egg whites which refuses to whip. One of the factors which makes egg whites reluctant to whip is evaporation.

If egg whites have to stand for any length of time, always cover the dish with several layers of dampened paper toweling followed by a piece of aluminum foil. This will prevent evaporation and keep the surface from skinning over. Always allow egg whites to warm to room temperature before attempting to whip them.

When any recipe calls for beaten egg whites, always wait until the last possible moment before beating. Let the egg whites stand at room temperature, unbeaten, but covered. If you beat the whites too soon before adding them to the recipe, they will lose their fluffiness and some of the white will drain back into the bottom of the bowl. Try as you may, it is impossible to rebeat this drain-back material.

When adding beaten egg whites to any mixture, always use a gentle folding motion; this preserves the air in the whites and the result will be a high and tender dish. If the egg whites are stirred into a mixture with too rough a touch, the result will be a flat, tough mixture.

Since the protein content of meals is the most expensive item, eggs, with their no-waste feature, can prove to be a real saving. That is, if they are properly stored and utilized.

Chapter III

EGGS FOR DINNER

BECAUSE MOST GOOD COOKS spend more planning time and money on dinner, it will be our first consideration.

Most homemakers only serve eggs for dinner in desperation. When caught short of time or supplies, eggs are turned to as a last resort.

With the high protein content of eggs, plus their minerals and vitamins, basing a meal around eggs is good reasoning and good family fare.

The delicate flavor and cheerful color of eggs can make a memorable dinner for your family. Start using eggs to replace other more expensive, protein-high foods in your dinners and you will win complete family approval.

SPINACH AND EGGS FLORENTINE STYLE

3 10-ounce packages frozen, chopped spinach, thawed
1 teaspoon salt
½ teaspoon pepper
12 eggs
½ cup grated Parmesan cheese
1 cup heavy whipping cream
1 teaspoon paprika

Divide each of the packages of spinach in half. Place each half in an individual, buttered casserole dish. Make an indentation in the center of the spinach. Sprinkle each portion of spinach with a portion of the salt and pepper. Sprinkle 1 teaspoon of Parmesan cheese over each portion. Reserve the remainder of the cheese.

Break each of the eggs into a saucer and slip two eggs on each portion of spinach without breaking the yolks. Spoon two tablespoons of cream over the eggs. Sprinkle each serving with some of the remaining Parmesan cheese.

Place in a 325° F. oven for 15 minutes or until the eggs are firm. Sprinkle a portion of the paprika over each of the eggs and serve at once, piping hot. Serves 6.

LITTLE KOREAN OMELETS

¼ pound very lean, double ground round steak
1 green onion, finely chopped; use a little of the green
1 clove garlic, finely chopped
2 tablespoons white sesame seed (available in most spice sections)
¼ teaspoon salt
2 tablespoons soy sauce
¼ cup peanut oil
6 eggs, beaten until slightly frothy
½ cup (additional) soy sauce
½ cup cider vinegar
¼ cup granulated sugar
1 tablespoon pine nuts, finely chopped (optional)

Mix the ground round steak, onion and garlic together. Set aside.

Place the sesame seed in a skillet over moderate heat. When the seeds begin to turn a golden brown and swell up, remove from the heat. Place the browned seeds in a bowl along with the salt and crush them with the back of a tablespoon. Add the crushed seeds, salt and 2 tablespoons of soy sauce to the meat mixture; mix well. Form the meat into ½-inch diameter meat balls.

Place 1 tablespoon of the oil in a large skillet over moderate heat and sauté the meatballs. Shake the pan back and forth so that the meatballs retain their round shape and are evenly browned.

Place another tablespoon of the oil in another large skillet or pancake griddle over moderate heat. Place 1 tablespoon of the eggs on the heated surface and allow it to spread out in a circle about 2½ inches in diameter. As soon as the edges become firm, place a meatball on one half the circle. Using a spatula, turn the other half of the egg circle over the meat ball. Press the edges slightly so that the runny portion of the circle completely seals the meat ball inside. Continue to sauté for a few seconds longer until the omelets are firm and golden brown. Place the omelets on an oven-proof platter in a 250° F. oven until you have used up all of the egg and meat balls.

Mix the additional soy sauce, vinegar and sugar together. Place in 6 individual little dishes. Sprinkle the top with a bit of the chopped pine nuts. Serve as a dip with the little omelets. Serves 6.

SHRIMP AND EGG CAKES

6 eggs, beaten until frothy
¼ teaspoon salt
½ teaspoon Accent
2 tablespoons soy sauce
1 cup green onion, thinly sliced; include a little of the green
¼ cup celery, thinly sliced
1 4-ounce can mushroom stems and pieces, coarsely chopped
1 7½-ounce can shrimp bits and pieces or ¾ cup chopped
    shrimp
2 tablespoons peanut oil

Sauce:
1 10-ounce can chicken broth
1 tablespoon soy sauce
¼ teaspoon granulated sugar
½ teaspoon (additional) Accent
2 tablespoons cornstarch

Mix the beaten eggs, salt, Accent, soy sauce, sliced green onion, celery, mushrooms and shrimp together well and set aside for 15 minutes to let the various flavors become united.

Heat the peanut oil over moderate heat in a large skillet or on a griddle. Drop tablespoonfuls of the egg mixture into the hot oil; allow them to form into lacy pancakes. Stir the egg mixture frequently so that the egg and solid ingredients are evenly mixed in each spoonful. Continue to cook the shrimp pancakes over moderate heat until the egg portions just begin to turn a golden brown and the tops are firm. Remove with a spatula and place on a heated platter in a 250° F. oven while you make the sauce.

Mix the chicken broth, soy sauce, sugar, Accent and cornstarch together well. Place over low heat and cook, stirring constantly, until glazed and thickened. Pour the hot sauce over the egg pancakes and serve at once. Serves 6.

EGGS ITALIAN

1 cup purple Italian onion, sliced ⅛ inch thick
½ cup soft butter
2 cups milk
8 hard-cooked eggs, sliced ¼ inch thick (see Chapter II)
2 tablespoons parsley, finely chopped
¼ cup grated Parmesan cheese
1 tablespoon lemon juice
½ teaspoon salt
¼ teaspoon freshly ground pepper
4 (additional) raw eggs, beaten until lemon yellow
3 medium-sized tomatoes, washed and sliced ½ inch thick (8 slices needed)
½ cup all-purpose flour
2 tablespoons olive oil
4 slices, toasted, enriched white bread, lightly buttered, or 2 English muffins, halved, toasted and buttered

Melt the butter in the top of a double boiler. Add the sliced onions and sauté over low heat until they are limp and transparent and just slightly browned. Add the milk and continue to cook over low heat until just below the scalding point. Remove from heat and stir in the sliced eggs, parsley, grated cheese, lemon juice, salt and pepper. Mix well.

Add ½ cup of the hot milk mixture to the beaten eggs and mix well; then add the beaten egg mixture to the hard-cooked egg mixture.

Place over slowly boiling water and cook, stirring constantly, until the mixture has thickened. Turn off the heat, cover and set aside while you prepare the tomatoes.

Dip the tomato slices in the flour. Place the olive oil in a skillet over moderate heat and sauté the tomato slices until they are a golden brown. Do not overcook, as they should retain their round shape. Place two browned, hot tomato slices on a slice of toast; then top with the hot, hard-cooked egg mixture. Serve at once. Serves 4.

EGG PANCAKE SUPPER

6 hard-cooked eggs, peeled (see Chapter II)
6 strips bacon, diced in ¼-inch cubes
¼ cup chopped green onion
¼ cup parsley, finely chopped
1 cup prepared pancake mix
1½ cups milk
⅓ cup melted butter
1 (additional) well-beaten egg
½ cup sour cream
¼ cup grated Parmesan cheese

Chop the hard-cooked eggs until they are the consistency of hamburger.

Place the bacon cubes in a skillet and sauté until they are crisp and golden brown. Remove the bacon cubes with a slotted spoon and drain on absorbent paper. Add the green onion to the remaining bacon fat and cook until slightly browned. Remove the onion with a slotted spoon and add to the chopped eggs along with the parsley and drained bacon cubes. Mix well. Mix the milk and the pancake flour; beat until free of lumps. Add the beaten egg and 1 tablespoon of the melted butter and mix again. Stir one half of the chopped egg mixture into the pancake batter. Set aside for 5 minutes for the flavors to unite.

Using the reserved bacon fat, fry large-sized pancakes, about 4 inches in diameter, on a hot griddle. As soon as the pancakes are golden brown on both sides, sprinkle with a portion of the remaining chopped egg mixture. Roll up the pancake jelly-roll fashion and place in a buttered, oblong, casserole dish. Place the rolled-up pancakes closely together; keep warm in a 250° F. oven until you have completed all the pancakes.

Brush the tops of the pancake rolls with the remaining butter and then spread the sour cream over the top. Sprinkle the surface with the grated Parmesan cheese. Return the dish to a 350° F. oven and bake for 10 minutes or until the cheese has melted and become slightly golden. Serve at once, piping hot. Serves 6.

EGG FOO YOUNG WITH SHRIMP

½ cup onion, coarsely chopped
1 clove garlic, finely minced
1 tablespoon peanut oil
1 cup cooked, deveined shrimp cut into ¾-inch pieces
6 eggs, beaten until slightly bubbly
½ teaspoon Accent
½ teaspoon salt
⅛ teaspoon freshly ground pepper
2 tablespoons (additional) peanut oil

Sauce:
¼ cup butter
¼ cup flour
1 teaspoon granulated sugar
2 chicken bouillon cubes dissolved in 1 cup boiling water
¼ cup soy sauce
1 cup canned bean sprouts, drained

Place the onion, garlic and oil in a skillet over moderate heat and sauté until the onion becomes limp and transparent. Add the pieces of shrimp and sauté them until they begin to turn a golden brown. Remove from the heat and allow to cool.

Mix the eggs, Accent, salt and pepper thoroughly. Add the shrimp and onion mixture and mix all well.

Place the additional peanut oil in a skillet which has a tightly fitting cover over low heat; add the egg mixture and cook very slowly, covered, until the eggs are firm. Fold in half and place on an over-proof platter under the broiler until a golden brown.

For the sauce, melt the butter in the same skillet. Stir in the flour until smoothly blended. Add the sugar, hot bouillon water and soy sauce. Cook over very low heat, stirring constantly, until the mixture has thickened. Add the bean sprouts and continue to cook a few seconds longer until heated through. Pour the sauce over the shrimp omelet and serve. Serves 6.

EGG CROQUETTES

8 hard-cooked eggs, chilled and peeled (see Chapter II)
1 4-ounce can mushroom stems and pieces, drained
½ teaspoon salt
¼ teaspoon pepper
3 tablespoons butter
3 tablespoons all-purpose flour
1½ cups milk
1 (additional) raw egg
¼ cup (additional) milk
1½ cups fine bread or cracker crumbs
Vegetable oil for deep frying
1 tablespoon parsley, finely chopped

Chop the eggs and mushrooms until they are the consistency of coarse corn meal. Add the salt and pepper and mix well.

Melt the butter in a saucepan over low heat; stir in the flour. When the mixture is smooth and free of lumps, add the milk and continue to cook over very low heat, stirring constantly, until the mixture is thick and creamy.

Add ½ cup of the thick cream sauce to the chopped eggs and mushrooms. Reserve the rest of the cream sauce until later. Mix the eggs, mushrooms and cream sauce together well and spread over the bottom of a flat pan. Place in the coldest part of the refrigerator for 1 hour to become firm and solid.

When chilled and firm, form the mixture into balls about the size of an egg. Beat the additional raw egg until frothy, add the additional milk; mix well. Dip each ball into the egg-milk mixture and then roll in the bread or cracker crumbs until completely covered.

Place the croquettes in the hot oil (375° F.) and fry until they are a golden brown. Remove from the oil and place on a paper towel to drain.

Reheat the remainder of the cream sauce over slowly boiling water in a double boiler. Serve the croquettes with a portion of the hot cream sauce. Sprinkle with the minced parsley for added flavor and color. Serves 4.

EGG, MUSHROOM, SPINACH MOLD

4 eggs, separated
2 10-ounce packages frozen, chopped spinach, thawed to room temperature
¼ cup butter
¼ cup all-purpose flour
½ cup half-and-half cream
½ teaspoon salt
¼ teaspoon pepper
¼ teaspoon grated nutmeg
1 10-ounce can mushroom stems and pieces
1 10-ounce can cream of mushroom soup
4 (additional) hard-cooked eggs (see Chapter II)

Beat the egg yolks until they are lemon colored. Set aside. Beat the egg whites until they stand in peaks. Set aside.

Melt the butter in a large skillet and add the flour; mix well and continue to cook until the mixture bubbles. Stir in the cream, salt, pepper and nutmeg. Continue to cook, stirring constantly, until the mixture is thick. Take two tablespoons of the mixture and add to the egg yolks. Mix well and then add the egg yolks to the cream mixture. Mix thoroughly and cook for a few seconds. Add the chopped spinach and mix until all is smoothly blended. Remove from the heat and allow to cool.

Fold the beaten egg whites into the spinach mixture, taking care to retain all of the air. Spoon the mixture into a 10-inch generously buttered ring mold. Place the mold, uncovered, in a pan of hot water in a 350° F. oven and bake for 35 minutes or until the mold is firmly set and slightly puffed up.

Meanwhile, heat the mushroom soup, just as it comes from the can, and the mushroom stems and pieces over rapidly boiling water in a double boiler. Five minutes before serving, add the sliced hard-cooked eggs to the mushroom soup and allow them to heat through.

Loosen the spinach ring with a sharp knife and unmold on to a heated platter. Pour the egg-mushroom soup mixture into the center. Serve piping hot. Serves 6.

VIENNESE POACHED EGGS

8 eggs
1 cup half-and-half cream
4 tablespoons butter
16 slices thin, lean bacon
8 slices enriched white bread
Salt and pepper to taste

For true Viennese-style Eggs, you should use a large European-style egg poacher. If you do not own one, these eggs can be made in individual custard cups.

Butter 4 poachers or custard cups lavishly. Place ¼ cup of the cream in each of the egg poacher cups over rapidly boiling water. When the cream has reached the scalding hot stage, break the eggs into a saucer, one by one, and slip two into each cup of hot cream. Cover and poach until the eggs are firm and slightly glazed over.

Broil the bacon until it is crisp and golden. Toast the slices of bread. Butter four of the slices and place in the oven to keep warm. Place the remaining unbuttered toast on four heated serving plates; top each piece of toast with four of the slices of crisp bacon. Top the bacon with two of the poached eggs and their hot cream. Season each serving to taste. Serve at once with buttered hot slices of toast. Serves 4, allowing 2 eggs per person.

EGG AND CLAM BAKE

6 eggs
4 cups coarse cracker crumbs
¼ cup onion, finely chopped
2 cups milk
2 7½-ounce cans minced clams, with their juice
¼ cup melted butter

Beat the eggs until they are thoroughly mixed and bubbly. Add the cracker crumbs, chopped onion and milk and mix again. Add the minced clams and their juice and stir until the clams are evenly distributed throughout the mixture.

Pour into a buttered baking dish, smooth down the surface and drizzle the melted butter over the top.

Bake in a 350° F. oven for 40 minutes or until the top is a delicate golden brown. Serve piping hot. Serves 6.

ENGLISH MUFFINS AND EGGS

6 eggs
½ teaspoon salt
¼ teaspoon freshly ground pepper
½ cup half-and-half cream
¼ cup soft butter
4 English muffins, split in half
½ cup catsup
1 cup grated mild American cheese

Beat the eggs with a fork or slotted spoon just enough to mix the yolk and whites; add the salt, pepper and cream. Beat again to mix well.

Melt the butter in the top of a double boiler and add the eggs. Cook over water which is just below the boiling point.

Meanwhile, lightly toast the English muffin halves under the broiler until they are a rich golden brown. Spread each muffin half with a portion of the catsup.

Stir the eggs from the sides of the double boiler until they begin to thicken and are scrambled but not dry.

Spoon a portion of the eggs on each half of the English muffin. Sprinkle the grated cheese over the eggs. Place the muffin halves, cheese side up, on a baking sheet. Broil about 6 inches from the heat until the cheese just begins to melt and becomes slightly bubbly. Serve at once, piping hot. Serves 8, allowing one muffin half per person.

EGG AND ASPARAGUS DINNER

1 #2 can asparagus spears, drained
6 hard-cooked eggs, peeled and sliced (see Chapter II)
½ cup grated mild Cheddar cheese
1 10-ounce can cream of asparagus soup
½ cup buttered bread crumbs

Divide the asparagus in half. Place half the spears over the bottom of a 2-quart casserole clock fashion. Arrange half the hard-cooked egg slices over the top of the asparagus. Sprinkle the eggs with the cheese. Spoon half the can of cream of asparagus soup over the top.

Repeat with the remainder of the asparagus spears, eggs and soup. Sprinkle the buttered bread crumbs over the top. Place in a 350° F. oven for 30 minutes. Serves 6.

HAM AND EGGS #1

8 eggs
¼ teaspoon salt
¼ teaspoon pepper
¾ cup half-and-half cream
1 cup boiled ham, diced in ¼-inch cubes
3 tablespoons butter
8 slices enriched white bread, toasted to a golden brown
¾ cup chili sauce
1 cup grated mild American cheese

Beat the eggs with a slotted spoon or fork just enough to mix the whites and yolks. Add the salt, pepper and cream. Beat again to mix well. Add the cubes of boiled ham.

Melt the butter in the top of a double boiler and add the egg mixture. Cover and cook over water which is just below the boiling point.

Stir the eggs from the sides of the double boiler when they begin to thicken and congeal. Continue to stir and cook until the eggs are scrambled but not dry.

Place a portion of the eggs on the slices of toast. Drizzle some of the chili sauce over each portion of eggs. Sprinkle with a portion of the cheese.

Place the toast, cheese side up, on a flat baking sheet. Broil about 6 inches from the flame until the cheese begins to melt and becomes bubbly. Serve at once, piping hot. Serves 8, allowing 1 open sandwich per person.

Variation:
Canned luncheon meat may be used in place of the boiled ham.

HAM AND EGGS #2

8 hard-cooked eggs (see Chapter II)
1 4½-ounce can deviled ham
1 tablespoon parsley, finely chopped
1 teaspoon dill pickle, finely chopped
1 10-ounce can Cheddar cheese soup
½ cup milk
1 tablespoon grated Parmesan cheese
1 tablespoon butter
¼ teaspoon paprika

Slice the eggs lengthwise and remove the yolks. Set the whites aside. Using a fork, mash the yolks until they are fine and smooth. Add the deviled ham, parsley and chopped dill pickle. Mix well. Using a table knife, stuff each half of the white with a generous portion of the mixture.

Place the filled eggs side by side in a buttered casserole dish. Mix the Cheddar cheese soup with the milk and beat with a whisk or beater until smooth. Spoon the soup mixture over and around the eggs. Sprinkle the surface with the Parmesan cheese. Place several dabs of the butter over the surface. Sprinkle with the paprika.

Place in a 350° F. oven for 25 minutes or until the surface is slightly browned. Serve at once with wedges of enriched white bread toast. Serves 6.

HAM AND EGGS #3

8 hard-cooked eggs, peeled and cut in ¼-inch slices (see Chapter II)
2 cups fine bread crumbs
2 cups lean cooked ham, finely chopped
1 10-ounce can cream of mushroom soup
1 cup light cream
¼ cup butter
¾ cup cracker crumbs, coarsely crushed

Cover the bottom of a well-buttered 2-quart casserole with half the slices of hard-cooked eggs.

Toss the bread crumbs and the chopped ham together until well mixed. Place half of this mixture over the sliced eggs.

Mix the mushroom soup and cream together until smooth; pour half of this mixture over the crumbs and ham.

Repeat, using the remainder of the eggs, ham and crumbs and soup mixture.

Melt the butter in a skillet over moderate heat and then add the cracker crumbs. Turn the crumbs over several times until they are evenly buttered and just beginning to turn a golden brown. Sprinkle the hot, buttered cracker crumbs over the top of the casserole.

Place the casserole in a 350° F. oven for 30 minutes or until heated through and the top is a rich golden brown. Serve at once, piping hot. Serves 6.

CHEESE AND EGG SCRAMBLE DINNER

12 eggs
1½ cups mild Cheddar cheese, finely grated
½ teaspoon salt
¼ teaspoon pepper
¼ cup half-and-half cream
¼ cup melted butter, cooled to room temperature
3 English muffins
12 strips lean bacon
1 4-ounce can mushroom stems and pieces, drained

Beat the eggs with a whisk or rotary beater until they just begin to get bubbly. Stir in the grated Cheddar cheese, salt, pepper and cream. Add half of the melted butter and mix well.

Place the remainder of the melted butter in the top of a double boiler over barely boiling water. Add the egg mixture. Cover and allow to cook at very low temperature for at least 10 minutes.

Meanwhile, split the English muffins in half and toast them lightly under the broiler. Cut the bacon into 1-inch squares and sauté until a light golden brown. Pour off half of the excess grease and add the mushrooms to the bacon. Continue to sauté until the mushrooms are heated through and just begin to brown on the edges. Place a portion of the bacon and mushrooms on top of each half of the English muffins. Place in the oven to stay warm until the eggs are done.

Stir the eggs from the edge of the double boiler and fold towards the middle until all are lightly scrambled. Place a portion of the scrambled eggs on top and around each of the bacon-topped muffins. Serve at once, piping hot. Serves 6, allowing 1 muffin half per person.

EGGS AND SAUSAGE MAIN DISH

16 links breakfast pork sausage
8 eggs
4 tablespoons melted butter
¼ cup parsley, finely chopped
4 slices enriched white bread, toasted and lightly buttered

Sauté the sausages until they are evenly browned and the outsides are crisp. Drain on paper toweling; then place four of the sausages in a circle in individual, buttered casserole dishes.

Break each egg into a saucer and slip two of the eggs into the circle of pork sausages. Take care not to break the yolks.

Place the casserole dishes in a 325° F. oven for 8 to 10 minutes or until the eggs are set but still soft. Pour a tablespoon of the butter óver each of the egg dishes and sprinkle with a portion of the parsley. Cut the toast into triangular wedges and place four wedges upright around the edge of the eggs. Serve at once, piping hot. Serves 4.

OYSTERS STEWED WITH EGGS

¼ cup butter
1 tablespoon onion, finely chopped
2 12-ounce cans stewing oysters
⅓ cup all-purpose flour
½ teaspoon salt
¼ teaspoon freshly ground pepper
1 cup milk
8 hard-cooked eggs (see Chapter II)
1 tablespoon parsley, finely chopped

Melt the butter in a 1-quart saucepan over low heat. Add the chopped onion and cook until the onion just begins to turn a golden brown.

Drain the oysters through a sieve; put liquid in a 1-cup measure. Add enough water to make 1 cup.

Stir the flour into the butter and onion mixture; stir until smooth. Add the oyster liquid and water. Continue to cook over low heat until slightly thickened. Stir about ¼ cup of the thickened mixture into the milk; mix well, then add the milk to the thickened oyster liquid. Add the salt and pepper and cook over low heat, stirring constantly, until thickened. Add the oysters and continue to cook over low heat until their edges begin to curl.

Slice the hard-cooked eggs into quarters lengthwise. Add them to the oyster mixture, stir lightly, and continue to cook over low heat for 3 minutes longer or until the eggs have become heated through. Just before removing from the heat, add the parsley.

Serve with plain boiled potatoes or over triangles of crisp buttered toast. Serves 4.

CHICKEN AND EGG CASSEROLE

2 7-ounce cans chicken white meat, slightly broken up, or 1¾
   cups chicken meat, coarsely chopped
1 10-ounce can clear chicken broth
1 cup half-and-half cream
8-eggs, beaten until frothy
½ teaspoon salt
⅛ teaspoon pepper
1 drop Tabasco sauce

Place the bite-sized pieces of chicken in the bottom of a
buttered casserole.

Mix the chicken broth and cream together in the top of a
double boiler over slowly boiling water. Heat until just below
the scalding point.

Pour the hot broth and cream mixture into the beaten eggs
a little at a time. Beat after each addition to prevent the eggs
from curdling. Add the salt, pepper and Tabasco sauce.

Pour the broth and egg mixture over the pieces of chicken.
Place in a 350° oven and bake for 1 hour or until a firm
custard has formed and the top is browned. Serve piping hot.
Serves 6.

Variations:
1 cup cooked fluffy rice may be added to this recipe for
   stretching. Sprinkle the cooked rice over the chicken pieces
   before adding the egg mixture.
1 cup cooked egg noodles, instead of the rice, may be added to
   this recipe for stretching. Arrange the cooked noodles over
   and around the chicken in the bottom of the casserole
   before adding the egg mixture.

WELSH-STYLE EGGS

2 cups mild Cheddar cheese, coarsely grated
12 eggs
Salt to taste
Seasoned black pepper (available in the spice section of most
   markets)

Butter 6 oven-proof dishes lavishly. Sprinkle ¼ cup of the
grated Cheddar in the bottom of each buttered dish.

Break the eggs in a saucer and then slip the egg over the

surface of the cheese. Take care not to break the yolk. Allow two eggs per dish. Sprinkle the remainder of the cheese over the surface of each dish. Sprinkle with salt and pepper to taste.

Place in a 325° F. oven for 20 minutes or until the eggs are fairly firm and just coated over. Serve at once.

Serve with wedges of buttered toast for dipping into the egg yolk and the melted cheese. Serves 6.

GOLDEN EGG SLICE DINNER

3 tablespoons butter or margarine
½ cup onion, finely chopped
3 tablespoons flour
1 very tiny pinch saffron
2 cups milk, scalded
8 hard-cooked eggs, peeled and sliced ¼ inch thick (see Chapter II)
4 slices toasted, enriched white bread, lightly buttered
¼ teaspoon paprika

Melt the butter in a saucepan over low heat. Add the chopped onion and sauté until the onion is limp and transparent. Stir in the flour; when smooth and free of lumps, add the pinch of saffron and the scalded milk. Cover and keep the mixture hot over barely boiling water in the double boiler.

Separate the circles of sliced egg yolk from the whites and add the yolks to the hot sauce. Stir the mixture well to break up the yolk circles slightly. Carefully fold in the slices of whites. Try not to break these up.

Cut the toast into triangular wedges and place on warm serving plates. Cover each slice of toast with a portion of the egg mixture. Sprinkle each serving with a bit of the paprika and serve at once. Serves 4 generously.

Variation:
Use whole wheat toast instead of white toast; whole wheat and the flavor of the saffron give this dish an entirely different flavor.

31

HAM AND EGG CASSEROLE

8 hard-cooked eggs, peeled and finely chopped (see Chapter II)
1½ cups chopped lean ham
1 tablespoon parsley, finely chopped
1 cup cracker crumbs
½ cup soft butter
3 tablespoons flour
2 cups milk
⅛ teaspoon pepper

Mix the finely-chopped eggs, ham and parsely together and set aside.

Place half the butter in a skillet over moderate heat and add the cracker crumbs. Sauté the crumbs until they are a golden brown and the butter is thoroughly mixed through them. Remove from the heat and set aside.

Place the remaining ¼ cup butter in a saucepan over moderate heat. When melted, stir in the flour until smooth. Gradually add the milk and the pepper; continue to cook over moderate heat, stirring constantly, until the sauce is thickened. Remove from the heat.

In a suitable buttered casserole, place ⅓ of the cracker crumbs over the bottom. Follow this with ⅓ of the ham and egg mixture and ⅓ of the cream sauce. Reserve a small portion of the crumbs for the top. Repeat the layers until you have used up all of the ingredients. Top with the reserved crumbs.

Place in a 350° F. oven for 25 minutes or until the top is a rich golden brown. Serve at once. Serves 6.

MEXICAN SCRAMBLED EGGS

8 eggs
2 green onions, sliced paper thin; include a little of the green
1 teaspoon chili powder
¼ cup catsup
2 tablespoons butter
1 6-ounce bag tortilla chips, slightly broken up

Beat the eggs until well blended. Add the onion, chili powder and catsup. Beat again until all is well mixed. Set aside.

Melt the butter in a skillet; add the tortilla chips and sauté over moderate heat until warmed through. Stir in the egg mixture and scramble until the desired consistency. Serve at once on heated plates. Serves 4 generously.

EGG BAKE DINNER

8 hard-cooked eggs, chilled and peeled (see Chapter II)
¼ cup mayonnaise
¼ teaspoon salt
¼ teaspoon curry powder
½ teaspoon prepared yellow mustard
1 8-ounce can mushroom stems and pieces, drained
1 10½-ounce can frozen cream of shrimp soup
1 10-ounce can cream of mushroom soup
½ cup grated mild American cheese
1 cup soft bread crumbs
2 tablespoons melted butter

Cut the eggs in half lengthwise. Remove the yolks to a bowl and set the whites aside. Mash the yolks until they are the consistency of coarse corn meal. Add the mayonnaise, salt, curry and mustard. Mix all together well. Heap a portion of the yolk mixture in the center cavity of each egg white half.

Place the egg white halves side by side in a suitable buttered baking dish. Sprinkle the drained mushroom pieces over and around the egg halves.

Place the mushroom soup and the frozen cream of shrimp soup in the top of a double boiler over rapidly boiling water. Cook, stirring frequently, until the two soups are thoroughly blended. Spoon the hot soup over and around the egg halves.

Sprinkle the cheese over the center of the dish. Mix the bread crumbs and melted butter thoroughly. Sprinkle the buttered crumbs around the outer edges of the dish.

Bake in a 350° F. oven for 20 minutes or until the cheese has melted and the dish is heated through. Serve at once. Serves 6.

PIQUANT SCRAMBLED EGGS

1½ cups tomato juice
1½ cups grated mild American cheese
8 eggs
½ teaspoon salt
¼ teaspoon freshly ground pepper
½ cup melted butter
32 saltine crackers

Place the tomato juice in the top of a double boiler over rapidly boiling water. Add the grated cheese and continue to cook until the cheese is melted. Lower the heat until the water is barely boiling.

Beat the eggs with a fork or rotary beater until the whites and yolks are mixed. Add the salt and pepper and mix well. Add the beaten eggs to the tomato and cheese sauce. Continue to cook over very low heat, stirring occasionally, until the eggs are scrambled.

Brush the saltine crackers with the melted butter and place in a 400° F. oven for 5 minutes or until the butter bubbles and the crackers turn a light, golden brown.

Place four of the toasted saltines on a plate and top with a portion of the tomato-egg mixture. Serve at once, piping hot. Serves 8.

By adding the eggs to the hot, cheese-tomato juice mixture they scramble separately, leaving a portion of the sauce mixture to top the saltines.

EGG, CHICKEN AND ALMOND SKILLET

2 7-ounce cans boned chicken white meat or 1¾ cups left-
    over chicken white meat
½ cup butter
¾ cup blanched, toasted almonds, finely chopped
¼ cup onion, finely chopped
2 drops Tabasco sauce
½ teaspoon chili powder
¾ cup half-and-half cream
1 chicken bouillon cube dissolved in ¼ cup boiling water
½ cup white wine
8 eggs
⅛ teaspoon pepper

Chop the chicken until it is the consistency of coarse corn meal. Set aside.

Place the butter in a skillet over moderate heat. Add the almonds and onion and sauté until the onion has turned a light golden brown. Stir in the chopped chicken. Add the Tabasco sauce, chili powder, cream, bouillon water and wine. Continue to cook over moderate heat, stirring constantly, until the liquid has almost completely evaporated.

Beat the eggs with a whisk or rotary beater until they are well blended. Stir the beaten eggs into the chicken-almond mixture. Continue to cook over low heat, stirring frequently, until the eggs are set and slightly glossy. Sprinkle the pepper over the top. Serve piping hot. Serves 6.

EGGS AND DEVILED HAM SUPREME

8 eggs
½ teaspoon salt
¼ teaspoon pepper
1 3-ounce can deviled ham, at room temperature
8 slices enriched white bread, toasted to a light golden brown
½ cup melted butter
1 10-ounce can cream of mushroom soup

Separate the eggs, keeping each yolk whole in the large end of the half shell which you used for separating. Place the yolks in their half shells back in the egg container so that they can be easily lifted out afterwards.

Beat the egg whites until they are stiff and stand up in shiny peaks. Add the salt, pepper and the deviled ham a little at a time. Fold in the deviled ham gently.

Brush the slices of toast with the melted butter. Mound a portion of the egg white and deviled ham mixture on top of each piece of buttered toast. Using the bowl of a tablespoon, make an indention in the top of each mound. Carefully slip the waiting egg yolk into this indention. Place the pieces of toast on a lightly buttered baking sheet in a 350° F. oven for 10 minutes or until the white begins to turn a delicate golden brown.

Heat the cream of mushroom soup (just as it comes from the can) in a double boiler over rapidly boiling water. Spoon a portion of the soup over each egg mound. Serve at once on heated plates. Serves 8.

35

RICE AND EGG BAKE

3 cups fluffy cooked rice
6 hard-cooked eggs (see Chapter II)
½ teaspoon salt
¼ teaspoon pepper
½ teaspoon powdered yellow mustard
1 cup grated mild American cheese
¼ cup onion, finely minced
¼ cup green pepper, finely chopped
1 8-ounce can tomato sauce

Place the cooked rice over the bottom of a 1½-quart, liberally-buttered casserole.

Slice the eggs in half lengthwise. Place the yolks in a mixing bowl along with the salt, pepper, mustard and ½ cup of the grated cheese. Mash all well with a fork until the mixture is smooth and creamy. Fill each cavity of the egg whites with a portion of the mixture, mounding up slightly. Make 12 indentations in the rice and place the filled egg halves in the indentations.

Mix the onion, green pepper and tomato sauce together and drizzle over the stuffed eggs and rice. Sprinkle the top of the casserole with the remaining ½ cup of cheese.

Place in a 375° F. oven for 20 minutes or until the cheese has melted and has become slightly bubbly. Serve at once. Serves 4.

ORIENTAL EGGPLANT WITH EGGS

3 small eggplants, about 3 inches in diameter at the widest part
1 teaspoon salt
½ cup all-purpose flour
½ cup peanut oil
6 eggs
½ cup scallion, finely chopped
½ cup soy sauce
1 tablespoon granulated sugar

Wash and peel the eggplants; slice ¾ inch thick, discarding the stem and the bottom end pieces. Sprinkle the slices with salt; place in a bowl, cover and set aside for ½ hour.

At the end of this ½ hour, pour off any liquid which has gathered around the eggplant slices; wipe each slice with paper toweling and then dip in the flour; coat each side well.

Heat ¼ cup of the oil in a 10-inch skillet over moderate heat. Sauté the slices of eggplant until they are a golden brown. Place the eggplant slices on a heated platter in a 200°F. oven while you prepare the rest of the dish.

Beat the eggs with a whisk until they are well mixed. Add the chopped scallion, soy sauce and sugar; mix well.

Place the remainder of the oil in the skillet and add the egg mixture. Cook over very low heat until the eggs begin to set. Using a fork, break up into small pieces after the egg mixture has become fairly firm.

Place the eggs over the sautéed eggplant and serve at once. Serves 6.

SCALLOPED EGGS

8-2-inch diameter firm tomatoes
8 eggs
¼ teaspoon salt
¼ teaspoon pepper
8 slices lean bacon
½ cup grated Parmesan cheese

Remove the stem end of the tomato with a sharp knife. Cut out the center portion of the tomato, leaving a cavity large enough to hold 1 egg. Reserve the cut-out portions.

Place the hollowed-out tomatoes in the bottom of a well-buttered, deep baking dish. Carefully break each egg and place in the hollow of the tomato. Sprinkle lightly with the salt and pepper. Place in a 375° F. oven for 10 minutes or until the egg is set and firm in the center of the tomatoes.

Chop the inside portions of the tomatoes quite finely. Sauté the bacon until it is crisp and golden brown. Drain on absorbent toweling and then crumble. Mix the bacon and the chopped tomato pulp. Place a spoonful of the mixture on top of each baked egg. Sprinkle each top with a portion of the Parmesan cheese.

Place under the broiler about 6 inches away from the heat until the cheese has just turned a golden brown. Serve at once, piping hot. Serves 8, allowing 1-tomato and egg combination per person.

EGG AND CRAB BAKE

6 eggs
2 8-ounce packages frozen Alaskan King Crab Meat, diced in
    ¼-inch cubes
1 cup celery, diced in ¼-inch cubes
1 cup grated sharp Cheddar cheese
1 cup mayonnaise
¼ teaspoon salt
⅛ teaspoon pepper
1 tablespoon Worcestershire sauce
2 tablespoons cooking sherry (optional)
1 cup soft bread crumbs
2 tablespoons melted butter

Beat the eggs until they are light and frothy. Add the diced
crab meat, celery, cheese, mayonnaise, salt, pepper, Worcestershire sauce and sherry. Mix all well and pour into a 1½-quart
buttered casserole.

Mix the bread crumbs and butter thoroughly and sprinkle
over the top of the casserole.

Bake in a 325° F. oven for 50 minutes or until a table knife
comes out clean when inserted in the middle of the dish. Serve
piping hot. Serves 6 generously.

Variation:

This dish is also excellent if made with cooked, deveined,
    cubed shrimp. Substitute 2 cups of diced shrimp for the
    crab meat.

ORIENTAL PORK AND EGGS

1½ pounds pork steak with bones removed, diced into ½-inch cubes
¼ cup white wine
½ cup soy sauce
1 stalk leek, about 1 inch in diameter at the bottom
6 1/16-inch thick slices ginger root
1 10-ounce can beef bouillon
¾ cup warm water
1 tablespoon granulated sugar
6 hard-cooked eggs, peeled (see Chapter II)

Sauté the pork cubes until they are a rich golden brown. Pour off all but 1 tablespoon of the accumulated fat. Add the wine and soy sauce and continue to cook over moderate heat until all the wine and soy sauce are absorbed by the meat.

Cut the leek up into 1-inch segments; then cut them in half lengthwise. Use a portion of the green. Add the leek, ginger root, bouillon, warm water and sugar. Stir to loosen any browned material in the bottom of the pan. Cover and cook at a slow simmer for ¾ of an hour.

Place the hard-cooked eggs in the gravy around the pieces of pork, cover again and cook for an additional ½ hour. Carefully turn the eggs over with a spoon once during this cooking period. They should be evenly colored with the pan gravy.

Remove the eggs to a heated platter; cut them in half lengthwise and spoon the pork and its sauce over and around the egg halves. Serves 6, allowing two egg halves per person.

Chapter IV

EGGS FOR LUNCH

WHEN TODAY'S BUSY homemaker is compelled to whip up a hot lunch at noon time, she is often hard pressed to come up with something tasty and nourishing.

If you are at an impasse when it comes to lunches, turn to the protein-perfect egg as your solution. Eggs in a noon lunch are light enough fare to permit afternoon mental activity instead of stifled, after-lunch yawns. Egg-based lunches contain enough protein to carry body demands over until dinner.

There are few foods that can be incorporated into a really good and good-for-you lunch as well as eggs. Try eggs to put that protein punch in your family's lunch.

EGGS AND SHRIMP LUNCHEON

2 tablespoons butter
2 tablespoons flour
1 cup milk
½ teaspoon salt
¼ teaspoon pepper
12 cooked, peeled, deveined shrimp
8 hard-cooked eggs, peeled (see Chapter II)
4 slices enriched white bread, toasted and lightly buttered

Melt the butter over moderate heat in the top of a double boiler. Stir in the flour and mix until smooth and bubbly. Add the milk and place over rapidly boiling water. Cook, stirring constantly, until the sauce is smooth and thick. Add the salt and pepper.

Cut the shrimp in half lengthwise and add to the hot cream sauce. Quarter the eggs lengthwise and add to the shrimp and cream sauce. Stir lightly and continue to cook over low heat until the shrimp and eggs are heated through.

Cut the toasted bread into four wedges, place on a heated plate and top with a portion of the creamed eggs and shrimp. Serve at once, piping hot. Serves 4.

EGG SANDWICH SPREAD

4 hard-cooked eggs, peeled (see Chapter II)
¼ cup soft butter
½ teaspoon salt
1/16 teaspoon red pepper
1 teaspoon Worcestershire sauce
1 teaspoon celery seed
1 tablespoon parsley, finely chopped
8 slices enriched white bread, lightly buttered

Chop the hard-cooked eggs until they are as fine as coarse corn meal. Add the butter and mix until smooth.

Add the salt, red pepper, Worcestershire sauce, celery seed and parsley; mix thoroughly.

Divide the mixture into 4 equal parts; spread 4 slices of the lightly-buttered bread with one part of the mixture. Top with the remaining four slices of bread. Press together slightly and cut into triangular shaped sandwiches. Serves 4.

This spread is also delicious served on cocktail crackers as an hors d'oeuvre.

EGG AND ONION PIE

6 hard-cooked eggs, peeled and sliced (see Chapter II)
3 onions 3 inches in diameter, peeled and sliced ¼ inch thick
⅓ cup butter
¼ cup all-purpose flour
1¼ cups milk
¼ cup grated mild American cheese
½ teaspoon salt
⅛ teaspoon pepper

Using 1 tablespoon of the butter, sauté the onion slices until they are limp and transparent. Spread the onion over the bottom of a lightly buttered casserole. Distribute the egg slices over the top of the onions. Set aside.

Melt the remainder of the butter in a saucepan. Stir in the flour; mix until smooth. Add the milk and cook over low heat, stirring constantly, until the mixture has thickened. Stir in the cheese, salt and pepper. Pour the sauce over the eggs and onions.

Place in a 350° F. oven for 15 minutes or until the top has turned a golden brown. Serve piping hot. Serves 6.

LITTLE PORK OMELETS

¾ cup roasted, lean pork, finely chopped
1 7½-ounce can shrimp, drained and finely chopped
¼ cup green onion, finely chopped
¼ cup chicken or beef broth
1 teaspoon cornstarch
2 tablespoons peanut oil
6 eggs, beaten until slightly frothy
1 tablespoon soy sauce
1 teaspoon granulated sugar
⅛ teaspoon ground ginger
⅛ teaspoon pepper
¼ teaspoon salt
¼ cup (additional) peanut oil

Mix the pork, shrimp and onion together thoroughly. Set aside and allow the flavors to blend for 15 minutes. Add the cornstarch to the broth, mix well and set aside.

Place the 2 tablespoons of peanut oil in a skillet over moderate heat and brown the pork, shrimp and onion slightly. Lower the heat and stir in the broth. Cook over low heat, stirring frequently, until the mixture has thickened and glazed. Remove from the heat and set aside.

Add the soy sauce, sugar, ginger, pepper and salt to the beaten eggs; mix well.

Place 1 tablespoon of the additional peanut oil in a skillet over moderate heat. Place 1 tablespoon of the egg mixture in the hot oil and allow it to form a circle; sauté until the edges begin to get firm. Place 1 teaspoon of the meat and shrimp mixture on one side of the egg circle; then fold over the other half. Press down the edges to seal. Continue to sauté the "half circles" until browned on both sides.

If using a large skillet or pancake griddle, you can make four of the omelets at a time. Replace the peanut oil as needed. After the omelets are browned, remove them to an oven-proof platter and place in a 250° F. oven until you have used up all of the ingredients. Serves 6.

Variations:

Add ¼ cup finely-chopped green pepper if you like the flavor;
  sauté along with the pork, shrimp and onions.
Use canned, drained, chopped lobster in place of the shrimp.
Use ¾ cup finely-chopped luncheon meat in place of the pork.
Add 1 tablespoon cooking sherry to the egg mixture for a
  different flavor.

WESTERN EGG ROLLS

4 eggs
¼ teaspoon salt
⅛ teaspoon pepper
8 strips bacon, diced in ¼-inch cubes
½ cup ground chuck or ground round steak
¼ cup green pepper, finely chopped
½ cup grated sharp Cheddar cheese

Beat the eggs until they are light and frothy. Add the salt
and pepper and mix well. Set aside.

Place the diced bacon in a skillet and sauté until it is crisp
and golden. Drain on absorbent toweling. Discard all but 1
tablespoon of the bacon fat.

Place the ground meat in the bacon fat and sauté until it
loses its reddish color and is just beginning to turn brown.
Remove from the heat and allow to cool slightly. Add the green
pepper and the grated cheese and mix well. Crumble the
drained bacon slightly and add it to the ground meat mixture.
Mix all well.

Heat a griddle until it is medium hot. Grease it lightly with
either butter or bacon fat. Again stir the egg mixture and pour
½ cup of the egg mixture into the center of the griddle. Allow
it to spread out. Cook about 1 minute and then turn over.
Place 2 tablespoons of the ground meat mixture on the
browned side and immediately roll up like a jelly roll. Do not
overbrown the second side as the eggs should not be over-
cooked. Serve the rolls at once, piping hot.

This recipe will make 6 rolls; allowing 1 roll per person,
serves 6.

EGG SURPRISE LUNCH

8 hard-cooked eggs (see Chapter II)
1 4-ounce can mushroom stems and pieces, drained
3 tablespoons tomato paste
3 tablespoons soft butter
3 tablespoons Parmesan cheese
½ teaspoon salt
¼ teaspoon freshly ground pepper
¼ pound (additional) butter
2 (additional) raw egg yolks (see Chapter XIII for using left-over whites)
¼ teaspoon (additional) salt
1 pinch cayenne pepper
1 tablespoon lemon juice
4 cups hot, cooked rice

Halve the hard-cooked eggs lengthwise and remove the yolks. Place the yolks and mushrooms in a chopping bowl; chop until the consistency of corn meal. Add the tomato paste, butter, cheese, salt and pepper and mix well. Fill each cavity of the egg whites with a portion of the mixture. Place the filled eggs on a pie tin, stuffed side up, in a 200° F. oven while you prepare the sauce and rice.

Divide the stick of butter into thirds. Place 1 portion of the butter and the raw egg yolks in the top of a double boiler over hot but not boiling water. Beat with a whisk until the butter has completely melted. As the mixture thickens, add another third of the butter and continue to beat. Add the remainder of the butter and continue to beat until the mixture has thickened. Add the salt, cayenne pepper and lemon juice and continue to beat with the whisk until smooth and creamy. Should the sauce separate, add two tablespoons of boiling water, a drop at a time, and continue beating until creamy.

Place a portion of the rice on four plates. Indent each portion with the back of a tablespoon. Place two of the heated, stuffed, egg halves in the indentation. Drizzle a portion of the hot sauce over the eggs and rice. Serve at once, piping hot. Serves 4.

Variations:

This dish may also be served over boiled, buttered noodles instead of rice.

This dish is also delicious served over fluffy, mashed potatoes instead of rice.

This dish is also excellent served over cooked, drained, chopped spinach.

EGGS AND TOMATOES

6 firm, ripe tomatoes 2½ inches in diameter
6 eggs
½ teaspoon salt
¼ teaspoon freshly ground pepper
¼ cup butter
2 tablespoons parsley, finely chopped
6 slices enriched white bread, toasted
¾ cup grated mild American cheese

Slice off the stem end of the tomato and discard. Using a teaspoon, remove the seeds and pulp from the tomatoes and set aside. Leave about ½-inch wall.

Place the tomato shells on a buttered baking sheet in a 400° F. oven for 5 minutes or until warmed through but not mushy.

Beat the eggs with a rotary beater or fork until the whites and yolks are well mixed. Chop the tomato pulp fairly fine and add it to the beaten eggs along with the salt, pepper and parsley.

Place the butter in the top of a double boiler over barely boiling water until it has melted. Add the tomato-egg mixture and continue to cook over barely boiling water until the mixture begins to thicken. Stir from the sides and the bottom of the double boiler until the entire mixture has scrambled. Spoon the scrambled egg and tomato mixture into the heated tomato shells.

Sprinkle a portion of the grated cheese over the surface of the toast. Place the egg-stuffed tomato in the center of each cheese-covered piece of toast. Place on a buttered baking sheet and return to a 400° F. oven for an additional 5 minutes or until the cheese has just begun to melt. Serve at once, piping hot. Serves 6.

EGG AND TOMATO LUNCH #1

4 firm ripe tomatoes, about 2½ inches in diameter
4 eggs
2 tablespoons butter
4 tablespoons soft bread crumbs
¼ cup parsley, finely chopped
1 teaspoon salt
½ teaspoon pepper

Cut the tops of the tomatoes off about ¾ of the way down. Using a grapefruit spoon, scoop out the stem portion of the tomato, leaving most of the seed sections intact.

Break each egg into a saucer and carefully slip the egg into the dug-out part of the tomato. Place a portion of the butter on top of each egg. Sprinkle the top of each egg with 1 tablespoon of the bread crumbs. Add the parsley. Top each with a portion of the salt and pepper.

Place the tomatoes on a greased baking dish and bake in a 350° F. oven for 15 minutes or until the egg is set but not hard cooked. Serve piping hot. Serves 4.

EGG AND TOMATO LUNCH #2

6 slices bacon
6 slices tomato, ½ inch thick and about 3 inches in diameter
½ cup all-purpose flour
6 eggs
6 slices toasted enriched white bread, lightly buttered

Sauce:
2 egg yolks (see Chapter XIII for use of left-over whites)
⅛ teaspoon salt
2 tablespoons lemon juice
¼ cup half-and-half cream
2 tablespoons butter

Sauté the bacon in a skillet over moderate heat until it is crisp and golden. Using a fork, remove the bacon to absorbent toweling. Retain the bacon grease in the skillet.

Dip the tomato slices in the flour and place them in the skillet over low heat. Sauté until they are slightly browned and warmed through. Turn off the heat and allow the tomato slices to remain in the skillet.

Poach the eggs in slightly salted water. Remove the poached eggs with a spoon or spatula and drain on absorbent toweling before slipping the egg off the spatula.

Place the slices of toast on an oven-proof platter. Top each slice of toast with a crumbled slice of the bacon; follow this with a slice of the sautéed tomato. Place the well-drained, poached egg on top of the tomato. Place the platter in a 225° F. oven to keep warm while you make the sauce.

Place the egg yolks in the top of a double boiler; add the salt and place over barely boiling water. Stir the yolks constantly; add the lemon juice and the half-and-half cream a little at a time. Continue to cook and stir until the mixture thickens. Remove the double boiler top from the hot water and add the butter in little lumps. Stir vigorously after each addition. Pour a portion of the sauce over the poached eggs, tomato and toast. Serve at once, piping hot. Serves 6.

EGG BALLS IN CHICKEN BROTH

1 46-ounce can clear chicken broth or approximately 2 quarts
   homemade chicken broth
1 4-ounce can boned chicken meat
4 hard-cooked eggs (see Chapter II)
2 (additional) raw eggs
¼ teaspoon salt
⅛ teaspoon freshly ground pepper
¼ cup all-purpose flour

This is a hurry-up luncheon which is both nourishing and satisfying.

Combine the chicken broth and the chicken meat in a 2-quart saucepan. Place over moderate heat until barely simmering; turn the heat back to simmer.

Chop the hard-cooked eggs until they are the consistency of corn meal. Beat the raw eggs until they are frothy and lemon colored; add the beaten eggs to the chopped, hard-cooked eggs. Add the salt and pepper and mix well.

Using the large end of a melon-ball maker, form into balls and then roll in the flour until coated. Drop into the simmering broth. Cover and simmer for 8 to 10 minutes or until the egg balls are firm and slightly puffed up. Serve in soup bowls, piping hot. Serves 4 generously.

ASPARAGUS AND EGG CURRY SAUCE LUNCH

¼ cup butter
½ cup chopped onion
½ teaspoon curry powder
1 10-ounce can cream of celery soup
½ cup milk
3 hard-cooked eggs, peeled and sliced (see Chapter II)
2 10-ounce packages frozen asparagus tips, cooked according
   to package directions and drained
¼ cup toasted chopped almonds

Place the butter in a saucepan over moderate heat. When the
butter has melted, add the chopped onion and the curry
powder. Continue to cook over moderate heat until the onion
is limp and transparent.

Add the cream of celery soup and the milk. Cook over low
heat, stirring constantly, until the soup is heated through and
thoroughly blended with the onion and butter. Add the sliced
eggs, stir lightly, and then remove from the heat.

Arrange the hot, cooked asparagus on a platter and pour the
sauce over it. Sprinkle the top with the toasted almonds.
Serves 6.

Variation:
Use canned bleached asparagus in place of the frozen tips.
   Place three large spears on pieces of toast and then top each
   portion with the sauce.

PIQUANT CREAMED EGGS

⅓ cup butter or margarine
⅓ cup all-purpose flour
2 cups milk
¼ cup parsley, finely chopped
1 teaspoon Worcestershire sauce
3 drops Tabasco sauce
½ teaspoon salt
¼ teaspoon pepper
8 hard-cooked eggs, sliced ¼ inch thick (see Chapter II)
4 English muffins, halved

Melt the butter or margarine in the top of a double boiler;
stir in the flour and continue to stir until smooth. Add the
milk and place over rapidly boiling water. Cook over boiling

water, stirring constantly, until the sauce is smooth and thick. Add 2 tablespoons of the parsley and mix well.

Stir in the Worcestershire sauce, Tabasco sauce, salt, pepper and sliced eggs. Reduce heat until the water is barely moving.

Place the English muffin halves under the broiler about 6 inches from the flame and toast the cut side until it is a delicate golden brown. Place two of the muffin halves on a heated plate and top with a portion of the egg mixture. Top with portion of remaining parsley. Serve piping hot. Serves 4.

ORIENTAL FRIED STUFFED EGGS IN SAUCE

6 hard-cooked eggs, peeled and chilled (see Chapter II)
½ cup lean boiled ham, finely chopped
½ cup English walnuts, finely chopped
¼ cup cornstarch
⅓ cup water
Vegetable oil for deep frying
1 10½-ounce can beef bouillon
¼ cup soy sauce
¼ teaspoon light brown sugar
2 tablespoons cooking sherry (optional but good)
¼ teaspoon salt

Halve the hard-cooked eggs lengthwise. Remove the yolks to a bowl and set the whites aside.

Mash the yolks with a fork until smooth; add the finely chopped ham and walnuts. Mix all thoroughly. Spread a portion of the yolk mixture in the cavity of each egg white.

Mix the cornstarch and water together until you have a smooth paste. Spread the cornstarch mixture over the filling of each egg.

Heat the vegetable oil to 350° F. and carefully place each egg half in the hot oil. Deep fry until a golden brown. Remove from the hot oil to absorbent toweling.

Place the beef bouillon, soy sauce, brown sugar, sherry and salt in a shallow pan which has a tightly fitting cover. Heat to just below the boiling point and add the fried eggs, filling side up. Cover tightly and simmer for 8 minutes or until heated through. Serve at once. Serves 6.

SUPER STUFFED EGGS

1 2¼-ounce can deviled ham
8 hard-cooked eggs, chilled and peeled (see Chapter II)
1 teaspoon parsley, very finely chopped
1 teaspoon piccalilli, pressed dry
1 tablespoon mayonnaise
¼ teaspoon paprika

Slice the hard-cooked eggs in half lengthwise; remove the yolks to a bowl and set the whites aside. Mash the yolks very fine with a fork. Add the deviled ham, parsley, piccalilli and mayonnaise.

Mix all until smooth. Using a table knife, refill the egg whites with the mixture. Sprinkle a little paprika over each of the stuffed eggs. Chill in the refrigerator for 1 hour or until firm. Serves 8, allowing 2 halves per person.

ORIENTAL SCRAMBLED EGGS

¼ cup peanut oil
¼ cup green onion, sliced paper thin; include a little of the green
1 7½-ounce can crab meat, drained; coarsely chop the large pieces
6 eggs
⅛ teaspoon ground ginger
1 tablespoon soy sauce
¼ teaspoon freshly ground pepper
½ teaspoon salt
¼ cup cooking sherry (optional)

Place the peanut oil in a skillet over moderate heat. Add the onion and sauté until slightly limp and transparent. Add the crab meat and continue to sauté until heated through. Reduce heat.

Beat the eggs until well mixed and slightly bubbly. Add the ginger, soy sauce, pepper, salt and sherry to the beaten eggs. Mix all well and pour into the hot crabmeat and onion mixture. Cook over low heat, stirring occasionally, until the eggs are scrambled.

Remove from the heat and serve on heated plates with toast. Serves 4.

SCRAMBLED EGGS WITH CORN

1 12-ounce can niblet corn, drained
¼ cup soft butter
½ teaspoon salt
¼ teaspoon freshly ground pepper
8 eggs

Melt the butter in a large skillet. Add the niblet corn, salt and pepper. Sauté until some of the kernels of corn begin to turn a golden brown.

Beat the eggs with a fork or rotary beater until the whites and yolks are mixed. Pour the beaten eggs over the corn and butter. Lower the heat and continue to cook until the eggs begin to get solid around the edges. Using a large spoon, turn the eggs occasionally until all are scrambled and firm. Serve at once, piping hot. Serves 4.

CHEESE AND EGG PUDDING LUNCH

10 slices enriched white bread
½ cup soft butter
1½ cups grated mild American cheese
4 eggs
2 cups milk
½ teaspoon salt

Remove the crusts from the slices of bread. Butter each slice of bread lightly. Stack into two piles 5 slices high. Using a very sharp knife, slice into 1-inch cubes.

Break up one pile of the buttered bread cubes and distribute them over the bottom of a well-greased baking dish. Sprinkle ½ cup of the cheese over the bread. Follow this with half of the remaining bread cubes and another ½ cup of cheese. Repeat, ending up with the last ½ cup of cheese over the top.

Beat the eggs until they are well mixed and frothy. Gradually add the milk and salt and continue to beat for a few seconds longer. Pour the egg and milk mixture over the bread and cheese without disturbing the layers. Allow the mixture to stand for 1 hour. Place in a 300° F. oven for 40 minutes or until the top is a golden brown. Serves 6.

QUICK EGGS BENEDICT

2 large-sized English muffins (4 inches in diameter)
¼ cup soft butter or margarine
4 slices lean boiled ham, ⅛ inch thick
8 eggs
1 10-ounce can cream of mushroom soup
1. 4-ounce can mushroom buttons, drained
Salt

Split the English muffins into halves the broad way. Remove any excess dough from the inside of the muffins, leaving about a ½-inch wall on the bottoms and sides. Butter the insides of the muffins.

Cut the slices of boiled ham into quarters. Arrange the quarters so they line the muffin halves, slightly overlapping in the center. Place the muffin halves, ham side up, on a cooky sheet and place in a 350° F. oven for 8 to 10 minutes or until the ham and muffins are heated through and the edges of the muffins are just beginning to turn a golden brown.

Heat the cream of mushroom soup in the top of a double boiler just as it comes from the can. Add the mushroom buttons and mix well. Cover and keep hot over barely boiling water.

In a large shallow skillet, bring enough slightly salted water to a boil to cover the eggs by about 1 inch. Break each egg into a saucer. Bring the edge of the saucer to the surface of the water and allow the egg to slip into the water quickly. After all the eggs have been placed in the water, turn the heat back until barely simmering. Poach the eggs at this low simmer until they reach desired firmness.

Remove the eggs from the water with a slotted pancake turner or large slotted spoon. While the egg is still on the turner or spoon, drain thoroughly on several layers of paper toweling. Place two of the poached eggs in the center of each of the ham-lined, hot muffins.

Place the muffins with the poached eggs on a heated serving plate and top each with a portion of the hot soup and mushroom mixture. Serve at once. Serves 4, allowing two eggs and 1 muffin half per person.

SALMON LOAF WITH EGGS

1 1-pound can salmon
3 eggs
½ cup milk
¼ teaspoon salt
⅛ teaspoon pepper
1 tablespoon onion, finely minced
1 teaspoon lemon juice
3 cups Special K cereal

Sauce:
¼ cup butter
¼ cup all-purpose flour
1 cup milk
¼ cup salmon liquid
3 (additional) hard-cooked eggs, peeled and finely chopped (see Chapter II)
1 tablespoon lemon juice
¼ cup parsley, finely chopped

Drain the salmon and reserve the juice. Remove any skin and bones and then flake the salmon quite finely with a fork.

Beat the raw eggs until they are light and lemon colored. Add the eggs to the flaked salmon along with the milk, salt, pepper, onion and lemon juice. Mix all thoroughly. Add the cereal and mix again. Place the mixture in a lavishly-buttered loaf pan; bake in a 325° F. oven for 1 hour.

Melt the butter in a saucepan; stir in the flour and cook over low heat until the mixture begins to bubble. Add the milk and the salmon liquid. Continue to cook over low heat, stirring constantly, until the mixture has thickened.

Remove the sauce from the heat and stir in the chopped eggs and lemon juice.

Loosen the salmon loaf with a sharp knife and invert on to a heated platter. Pour the egg sauce over the loaf. Garnish the top with the finely-chopped parsley. Cut into generous slices and serve each slice with a portion of the sauce. Serves 6.

DOUBLE DEVILED EGGS

8 hard-cooked eggs, chilled and peeled (see Chapter II)
¼ cup mayonnaise
1 teaspoon onion juice
1 teaspoon yellow prepared mustard
½ teaspoon A-1 Sauce
1 2¼-ounce can deviled ham
⅛ teaspoon freshly ground pepper
16 sprigs parsley

Cut the eggs in half lengthwise. Place the yolks in a bowl and set the whites aside.

Mash the egg yolks with a fork until they are the consistency of coarse corn meal. Add the mayonnaise, onion juice, mustard and A-1 sauce. Mix all well and then add the deviled ham and pepper and mix again.

Mound up a portion of the mixture in each of the waiting egg white halves. Refrigerate at least 30 minutes. Place a sprig of parsley in the center of each egg and serve. Serves 8, allowing two egg halves per each serving.

MIMOSA EGGS

6 hard-cooked eggs, peeled (see Chapter II)
1 cup mayonnaise
2 tablespoons minced parsley
6 slices enriched white bread, toasted

Preheat the oven to 350° F.

Spread ¼ cup of the mayonnaise over the bottom of a pie pan with a rubber spoon. Sprinkle 1 tablespoon of the minced parsley over the mayonnaise.

Cut the eggs in half lengthwise. Place the halves, yolk side down, in the piepan. Spread the remainder of the mayonnaise over the tops of the eggs and sprinkle with the remaining tablespoon of parsley.

Place the eggs in the preheated 350° F. oven for 5 minutes or until the mayonnaise just begins to bubble. Serve at once by placing two egg halves on a slice of the toast, top with a portion of the hot mayonnaise. Serves 6.

EGG AND POTATO MEAL

4 large, baked Idaho potatoes (can be left-over potatoes)
¼ cup scalded milk (cream is even better)
¼ cup butter
½ teaspoon salt
¼ teaspoon pepper
8 eggs
¼ cup parsley, finely chopped

Cut the baked potatoes in half lengthwise. Scoop out the potatoes, leaving wall a ¼ inch thick. Mash the scooped-out potato finely. Add the scalded milk and butter a little at a time while mashing. Add the salt and pepper and continue to whip and mash until the potato is light and fluffy. If the potatoes were baked very dry, increase the amount of scalded milk.

Fill each potato shell half with a portion of the mixture. With the back of a tablespoon, make an indention in the top of each filled potato. Place the potatoes in a baking pan. If the potatoes are inclined to tip or tilt in the baking pan, wedge them in place with wads of crumbled aluminum foil.

Break the eggs in a cup and then carefully slip them into the indentation. Sprinkle each with a bit of parsley.

Place in a 350° F. oven for 10 minutes or until the egg is firm and set. The eggs should be fairly soft so that the yolk serves as a built-in gravy for the potato and its shell. Serve at once, piping hot. Serves 4.

EGGS AND TOMATOES, ORIENTAL STYLE

6 eggs, beaten until frothy
½ teaspoon Accent
½ teaspoon salt
¼ teaspoon granulated sugar
¼ cup peanut oil
3 3-inch diameter fresh tomatoes, cut into eighths from top to bottom

Mix the beaten eggs, Accent, salt and sugar together well. Heat the peanut oil in a large skillet over moderate heat and then add the egg mixture.

When the eggs begin to congeal around the edges, stir in the tomato pieces and continue to cook for 3 minutes longer or until the eggs have set. Serve at once, piping hot. Serves 6.

EGGS IN INDIAN CURRY

¼ cup butter
¼ cup onion, finely chopped
¼ cup flour
½ teaspoon curry powder
2 cups chicken broth
¼ cup whipping cream
8 hard-cooked eggs (see Chapter II)
1 tablespoon chutney (optional but good)
1 small firm tomato
1 small tart apple, peeled and cored
4 cups hot, cooked rice
¼ cup toasted almond slivers

Melt the butter in the top of a double boiler; add the chopped onion and sauté until the onion is transparent and limp. Stir in the flour mixed with the curry powder and mix until smooth and slightly bubbly. Mix the chicken broth and the cream together; then gradually add to the onion mixture. Place over rapidly boiling water and cook, stirring constantly, until the mixture has thickened. After it has thickened reduce the heat to barely simmering, cover and allow to cook while you prepare the remainder of the ingredients.

Chop the peeled, hard-cooked eggs, chutney, tomato and apple very coarsely and add to the curry sauce. Continue to cook over low heat for an additional 8 minutes or until all is warmed through.

Serve over portions of the hot cooked rice; garnish with a sprinkle of the almond slivers. Serves 4.

DEVILED EGG LUNCHEON

4 hard-cooked eggs, peeled (see Chapter II)
¼ teaspoon salt
1 teaspoon grated horseradish, pressed dry
1 tablespoon Roquefort cheese
1 tablespoon heavy cream
1 10-ounce can cream of mushroom soup
1 4-ounce can mushroom stems and pieces, drained
½ cup (additional) heavy cream
4 slices enriched white toast, lightly buttered

Cut the eggs in half lengthwise and place the yolks in a bowl. Set the whites aside.

Add the salt, horseradish, Roquefort cheese and tablespoon of cream to the yolks. Mash with a fork until thoroughly mixed.

Spoon the yolk mixture back into each of the egg white halves.

Mix the mushroom soup, mushroom stems and pieces and cream in the top of a double boiler. Cook over rapidly boiling water, stirring frequently, until heated through.

Cut the pieces of toast in half diagonally and place one half of a stuffed egg on each triangle of toast. Spoon the hot mushroom sauce over the egg and toast. Serves 4, allowing two toast triangles and two egg halves per person.

DEVILED EGGS

8 hard-cooked eggs (see Chapter II)
1 teaspoon lemon juice
½ teaspoon powdered mustard
¼ cup mayonnaise
¼ cup melted butter
¼ teaspoon thyme
½ teaspoon salt
¼ teaspoon cayenne pepper
½ cup golden brown buttered bread crumbs
¼ cup parsley, finely chopped
½ teaspoon paprika

Slice the hard-cooked eggs in half lengthwise. Place the yolks in a mixing bowl and mash well. Add the lemon juice, powdered mustard, mayonnaise, melted butter, thyme, salt and cayenne pepper and mix until smooth.

Using a table knife, fill each cavity of the egg white with the yolk mixture. Mound up slightly.

Mix the bread crumbs, parsley and paprika together. Dip the top of each filled egg into the mixture. Place in the refrigerator to chill for about ½ hour. Serve with German or mayonnaise potato salad. Serves 8, allowing two halves of an egg per person.

EGG CUPS

4 slices enriched white bread
4 tablespoons butter
3 tablespoons (additional) butter
3 tablespoons all-purpose flour
2 cups milk
½ teaspoon salt
⅛ teaspoon pepper
1 teaspoon Worcestershire sauce
¼ cup grated Parmesan cheese
1 tablespoon grated Swiss Cheese
1 7-ounce can chicken white meat, finely chopped
4 eggs

Butter the slices of bread on both sides and place·in individual oven-proof dishes. Press the bread down into the dishes so that it forms a cup. Place in a 350° F. oven for 5 minutes or until a golden brown. Remove and set aside.

Melt the additional butter in a saucepan over low heat; stir in the flour; continue to stir until all is smooth. Add the milk, salt and pepper. Continue to cook over very low heat, stirring constantly, until thickened. Divide the thickened sauce in half.

To one half of the sauce add the Worcestershire sauce and the chopped chicken. Place a portion of this mixture over the toast. To the remainder of the sauce, add the grated Parmesan and Swiss cheese. Mix well and set aside.

Poach the eggs in slightly salted water. Drain the eggs and place on top of the chicken and cream sauce. Top this with a portion of the cheese-flavored sauce.

Place the dishes in a 350° F. oven for 8 minutes or until the top has turned bubbly and a light golden brown. Serve at once. Serves 4.

CLAM AND CORN FRITTERS

2 7½-ounce cans minced clams, undrained
6 eggs, beaten until lemon yellow
1½ cups all-purpose flour
2 teaspoons baking powder
½ teaspoon salt
¼ teaspoon pepper
1 12-ounce can vacuum-packed corn niblets, drained

Place the clams in a mixing bowl; stir in the beaten eggs. Sift the flour, baking powder, salt and pepper together twice; add to the clams and eggs. Mix well so that you have a smooth batter.

Fold in the corn niblets. Fry as you would pancakes on a hot, well-greased griddle using about ¼ cup of the mixture for each fritter. Serve piping hot with thin chips of iced butter on the side. Serves 6.

FLORENTINE EGGS

2 10-ounce packages frozen, chopped spinach, cooked according to package directions and drained
¼ cup butter
¼ cup all-purpose flour
2 cups milk
½ teaspoon salt
¼ teaspoon freshly ground pepper
½ cup grated Swiss cheese
½ cup grated Parmesan cheese
2 egg yolks (see Chapter XIII for using left-over whites)
8 whole eggs

Melt the butter in a saucepan over low heat; stir in the flour and continue to cook over low heat until smooth and bubbly. Gradually add the milk and continue to cook and stir until smooth and thickened. Add the salt, pepper, Swiss cheese and Parmesan cheese. Mix well and continue to cook for 3 minutes longer, stirring constantly, until the cheese has melted and is well blended into the sauce. Beat the egg yolks until they are lemon yellow. Add a few spoonfuls of the hot sauce to the yolks and then add the yolks to the sauce and mix well. Continue to cook over low heat for an additional 3 minutes, stirring constantly. Remove from the heat and set aside.

Divide the drained cooked spinach into 4 equal parts and place it over the bottom of buttered individual casserole dishes. Reserve 1 cup of the sauce. Spread ¼ of the remaining sauce over each of the spinach-filled casserole dishes. Break the eggs into a saucer and then slip two over the top of the spinach and the sauce in each dish. Spoon an additional ¼ cup of the sauce over the eggs, taking care not to break the yolks. Place the casserole dishes in a 250° F. oven for 10 minutes or until the top is bubbly and the eggs are firm. Serve at once. Serves 4.

NEAPOLITAN EGGS

¼ cup butter
2 cloves garlic, cut into thin slices
1 10-ounce can mushroom stems and pieces, drained
¼ cup onion, finely chopped
¼ cup all-purpose flour
2 cups hot beef broth or 1 10-ounce can beef bouillon plus
  ¾ cup water
½ cup dry white wine
½ teaspoon salt
¼ teaspoon pepper
8 hard-cooked eggs (see Chapter II)

Melt the butter in a saucepan over moderate heat. Add the garlic pieces and sauté until they begin to turn a delicate shade of brown. Remove the garlic pieces from the butter and discard. Add the mushroom stems and pieces and the chopped onion; sauté over moderate heat until they begin to brown around the edges and the onion is transparent and golden. Push the mushrooms and onions to one side and add the flour. Mix until smooth and free of lumps. Add the hot beef broth, mix well and continue to cook over moderate heat for 5 minutes until slightly thickened. Stir frequently.

Reduce the heat to just barely simmering and add the wine, salt and pepper. Continue to cook over low heat for an additional 8 minutes, stirring frequently.

Carefully remove the white portion of the hard-cooked eggs by just slicing up to the yolk but not through it. Retain the yolks in their round shape. Cut the egg whites up into ⅛-inch strips. Add the strips of egg white and the whole egg yolks to the hot sauce.

Mix all gently so you do not mash the egg yolks. Continue to cook over low heat for an additional 5 minutes or until the egg yolks are warmed through. Serve at once, piping hot. Serves 4.

Chapter V

EGGS FOR BREAKFAST

A NUTRITIONALLY SOUND breakfast should have protein in it. Eggs are a complete and perfect protein, containing all the amino acids essential for the building and maintaining of body tissues. In addition, eggs are rich in vitamins.

Eggs make the ideal breakfast because they keep you full of energy and pep until lunch.

Preparation of an egg-based breakfast is usually fast and easy. Eggs which are soft cooked, hard cooked, fried or poached make a good stable breakfast. They are also easily digested.

If you have strenuous objectors to eggs for breakfast, try some of the different recipes in this chapter; chances are you will get requests instead of rejects from now on.

EGG IN THE HOLE

4 slices enriched white bread
½ cup melted butter
4 eggs
Salt and pepper to taste

Using a round cooky cutter or a glass tumbler, cut a circle out of the center of each slice of bread. Reserve the centers.

Melt the butter over moderate heat in a skillet large enough to hold all the pieces of bread lying flat. Place the slices of bread in the melted butter and sauté them until golden brown on one side.

When done, turn the bread over; carefully break an egg in the center hole of each slice. Cover the skillet and continue to cook for 3 to 5 minutes or until the egg is firm and the top of the yolk is slightly coated.

Using a broad spatula, remove the egg and bread to a heated plate. Season to taste. Place the cut-out circles of bread in the skillet in the remainder of the butter and brown them quickly on each side. Serve the toasted circles with each egg in the hole. Serves 4, allowing 1 egg in the hole per person.

EGG AND POTATO BREAKFAST

6 eggs
4 medium-sized cold boiled potatoes (can be left-overs)
¼ cup butter
½ teaspoon salt
⅛ teaspoon freshly ground pepper

Coarsely grate or chop the potatoes. If the potatoes are rather overdone, chopping is best. They should be the size of peas.

Melt the butter in a skillet which has a tightly fitting cover; spread the potatoes over the bottom of the skillet in the melted butter. With the back of a tablespoon, make six indentations in the potatoes. Break an egg into each of the indentations. Season with salt and pepper.

Cover tightly and place over low heat; sauté until the eggs are firm and the potatoes are a slight golden brown on the bottom. Serve at once on heated plates. Serves 6, allowing one egg per person.

The moisture given off by the potatoes while they sauté rises up and cooks the eggs in this recipe, and that is why no definite time limit for cooking is given. A tightly fitting cover is necessary so that this moisture does not escape.

SCRAMBLED EGGS AND DRIED BEEF

1 6-ounce package dried beef, finely snipped
8 eggs
½ cup half-and-half cream
1 teaspoon parsley, finely chopped
¼ cup melted butter or margarine

Break the eggs into a bowl and beat with a whisk or rotary beater until they are well blended. Add the snipped dried beef, cream and parsley. Mix all well and set aside.

Place the melted butter in the top of a double boiler over slowly boiling water. Swirl the butter up around the sides of the double boiler to prevent the eggs from sticking.

Pour the egg mixture into the double boiler, cover and cook for 10 minutes or until the bottom begins to congeal. Stir the eggs gently until they reach desired firmness.

Serve piping hot on heated plates. Serves 6.

EGG AND SOUR CREAM SCRAMBLE

6 eggs
½ cup thick dairy sour cream
½ teaspoon salt
⅛ teaspoon freshly ground pepper
¼ teaspoon prepared yellow mustard
3 tablespoons butter

Beat the eggs until just broken up and mixed. Add the sour cream, salt, pepper and mustard and beat again until thoroughly mixed.

Melt the butter in a skillet over moderate heat until it just begins to sizzle. Add the egg mixture, lower the heat and cook until the edge begins to thicken. Stir from the edges and the bottom as the eggs become firm. When the eggs are firm, but not dry, transfer to a heated platter and serve. Serves 4.

FRIED EGGS, ITALIAN STYLE

6 eggs
¼ cup virgin olive oil
Salt and pepper to taste

If you have never had an egg sautéed in good olive oil, your taste buds are missing a real thrill. The selection of the olive oil for frying the eggs is most important. The olive oil should be from the first pressing; the flavor of this type oil is usually sweeter and more delicious than some of the cheaper grades which come from subsequent pressings.

Heat the olive oil over low heat in a skillet which has a tightly fitting cover. When the oil separates and runs to the edges of the pan, break each egg into a saucer and slip it carefully into the hot oil. Sprinkle all the eggs with salt and pepper to taste.

Cover tightly and cook over very low heat for 4 minutes or until the eggs are set; the white should be firm and the yolk shiny and slightly coated. Carefully transfer the eggs to a large heated platter or to individual plates and serve at once.

Buttered toast is excellent with this dish; however, if you want to be completely Italian, fry some slices of white bread in the remaining olive oil until they are a delicate golden brown. Serves 6, allowing 1 egg per person.

BREAKFAST BEEF AND EGG SCRAMBLE

1 6-ounce jar dried beef
1 cup boiling water
2 tablespoons butter
6 eggs
⅛ teaspoon freshly ground pepper
¼ cup milk

Snip the dried beef into ⅛-inch strips with a kitchen shears.
Pour the boiling water over the beef and let stand for 1
minute. Drain through a fine sieve. Press against the bottom
and sides of the sieve to remove all the water.

Melt the butter in a skillet over moderate heat until it is
sizzling. Add the dried beef and sauté over moderate heat
until the beef is slightly crisp.

Beat the eggs at low speed or with a fork until the whites
and yolks are evenly mixed. Add the pepper and milk and
continue to beat until mixed thoroughly. Pour the eggs over
the sautéed dried beef. Turn the heat back to very low. Cook,
stirring occasionally, until the eggs are firm but not dry.
Place on a heated platter and serve at once. Serves 4.

EGGS IN A CLOAK

6 eggs, separated
¼ cup butter
1 tablespoon parsley, finely chopped
½ teaspoon salt
⅛ teaspoon pepper

Using half of the butter, grease a 10-inch round baking
dish. Slip the yolks into the buttered baking dish; tilt the dish
from side to side so that they spread evenly over the bottom.
Dot the yolks with the remainder of the butter.

Beat the egg whites until they just begin to stand in peaks.
Add the parsley, salt and pepper and beat for 1 second longer.

Using a rubber spoon, gently spread the egg white mixture
over the yolks. Place in a 350° F. oven for 5 minutes or until
the whites are a delicate golden brown. Serve at once, piping
hot. Serves 6, allowing 1 egg per person. Serve with toast or
hot buttered muffins.

EGGS AND SAUSAGE

6 hard-cooked eggs, peeled and chilled (see Chapter II)
1 pound pork sausage meat
1 raw egg
1½ cups grated bread crumbs
Hot oil for deep frying

Cover each hard-cooked egg with about a ½-inch wall of the pork sausage meat. Pack and form firmly around the egg.

Beat the raw egg until it is light and bubbly. Dip each sausage-covered egg in the beaten raw egg and then roll in the crumbs. Press the crumbs firmly in place.

Heat the oil to 350° F. or until a cube of bread will brown in 1 minute. Using a spoon, carefully place each coated egg in the hot fat and fry until the outside is a rich golden brown. Remove from the fat and drain on paper toweling.

Cut each covered egg in half lengthwise and serve on a heated platter. Serves 6, allowing 1 egg per person.

CROUTON EGGS

4 slices enriched white bread
½ cup butter
8 eggs
Salt and pepper to taste

Dice the slices of bread into ½-inch squares. Melt the butter in a large skillet and place the bread cubes in the melted butter. Sauté, turning frequently, until they are crisp and a rich golden brown on all sides.

Place the toasted bread cubes in equal portions in 4 shallow, oven-proof dishes. Break each egg in a saucer and carefully slip two eggs into the dishes containing the toasted bread cubes. Season to taste with a little salt and pepper.

Bake in a 325° F. oven for 15 minutes or until the eggs are set and done to the desired firmness.

Serve at once. Serves 4, allowing 2 eggs per serving.

THREE-MINUTE BREAKFAST EGGS
WITH SALTINES

4 tablespoons butter
8 eggs at room temperature
12 saltines
Salt and pepper to taste

Place 4 oven-proof dishes or custard cups in the oven at 250° F. As soon as they are warm, place a tablespoon of butter in the bottom of each.

Place the eggs in a pan of cool water with about ½ inch of water over the top of the eggs. Place over moderate heat until the water begins to boil. Turn the heat back to simmer, cover and allow the eggs to cook for exactly three minutes. Remove from the burner and plunge the eggs under cold water for a second or two to stop the cooking action.

Coarsely crumble 3 of the saltines into each of the heated custard cups containing the melted butter. Break two of the soft-cooked eggs over the cracker crumbs and mix well. Salt and pepper to taste. Serve at once, piping hot. Serves 4, allowing 2 eggs per person.

This recipe is usually a favorite with children, who often seem to dislike any runny portions of an egg. The crackers absorb this runny portion and add a wonderful flavor to the eggs.

PROTEIN-RICH BREAKFAST

4 eggs
4 slices enriched white bread
½ cup soft butter
¼ teaspoon salt
⅛ teaspoon pepper
4 slices mild American cheese, 3 x 3 x ⅛ inch thick
⅓ cup catsup
8 slices bacon, grilled to a golden brown

Using a cooky cutter or a water tumbler, cut a circle approximately 2 inches in diameter from the center of each slice of bread. You can use the cut-out portion for bread crumbs in some other recipe. Butter the outer rim of the bread lightly on both sides. Put the bread in a large skillet which has a tightly fitting cover, place over low heat. Put a portion of the remaining butter in the hole in each piece of bread.

When the butter has melted, break the eggs, one by one, in a saucer and slip each into its circle of bread. Sprinkle each egg with a portion of the salt and pepper. Cut the cheese slices up into quarters and overlap the pieces on top of each egg. Top the cheese with 2 tablespoons of the catsup; place two slices of the grilled bacon over the cheese and catsup.

Cover the skillet tightly and allow to cook for 8 minutes or until the egg is firm and the cheese has melted. Serve piping hot. Serves 4.

POTATOES AND EGGS

2 large baked, left-over Idaho potatoes
4 tablespoons butter
4 tablespoons heavy cream
½ teaspoon salt
⅛ teaspoon pepper
4 slices boiled ham, 4 x 6 x 1/16 inch thick
4 eggs
1 10-ounce can cream of mushroom soup

Cut the baked potatoes in half lengthwise. Scoop out the insides, leaving a ½-inch wall. Place the scooped-out potato in a mixing bowl and chop up as you would for hash-browned potatoes. Add the butter, cream, salt and pepper. Mix well.

Fold the boiled ham slices in half the short way and place in the bottom of the potato shells. Press down well and add ¼ of the chopped potato mixture to each shell. Make an indentation in the middle and slip one of the eggs into each of the indentations. Place ¼ of the cream of mushroom soup on top and around the sides of each egg. Take care not to break the yolk. Place the potato halves in a greased baking dish. Bake in a 325° F. oven for 10 minutes or until the eggs are firm and the potatoes are warmed through. Serve at once. Serves 4.

BAKED BACON AND EGGS

¼ cup butter
6 slices enriched white bread, crusts removed
6 slices very lean bacon, diced into ¼-inch squares
6 eggs
½ teaspoon salt
⅛ teaspoon pepper

Melt the butter in a skillet; cut the bread up into ¾-inch cubes and place in the melted butter. Sauté the bread, turning frequently, until it is golden brown and crisp on all sides. Place the sautéed bread in a greased 1-quart casserole.

In the same skillet, sauté the bacon squares until golden brown and just beginning to get crisp. Remove the bacon cubes with a slotted spoon and drain them on paper toweling.

Beat the eggs until they are bubbly and well mixed. Add the salt, pepper and bacon cubes. Mix thoroughly. Pour over the crisped bread cubes. Place in a 325° F. oven and bake for 10 minutes or until the dish is the consistency of soft scrambled eggs. Serve piping hot. Serves 6.

Variation:
Substitute ¾ cup cubed ham or canned luncheon meat for the bacon; sauté in 1 tablespoon of butter until golden brown.

EGG PIE FOR BREAKFAST

4 slices enriched white bread
4 cups milk
½ teaspoon powdered mustard
4 raw eggs
4 hard-cooked eggs, peeled and sliced (see Chapter II)
½ teaspoon salt
⅛ teaspoon black pepper

Cut the bread up into 1-inch cubes. Mix the milk and powdered mustard together well. Beat the four raw eggs until they are light and lemon colored. Add the eggs to the milk. Add the salt and pepper and mix all well.

Place the bread cubes in the bottom of a 2-quart, lavishly buttered casserole. Distribute the hard-cooked egg slices over the top of the cubed bread.

Pour the milk and egg mixture over all. Bake in a 350° F. oven for 40 minutes or until the top is firm and a light golden brown. Serve piping hot. Serves 6.

FOOLPROOF SCRAMBLED EGGS

If you have trouble scrambling eggs, or if your scrambled egg dishes turn out too dry and broken apart, try this method. It is foolproof; another nice feature of making scrambled eggs in this manner is that they can be kept well up to an hour.

8 eggs
½ teaspoon salt
½ cup milk
¼ cup melted butter, cooled to room temperature

Break the eggs into a large earthenware bowl. Avoid using a plastic bowl, for plastic seems to discourage the fluffy beating of eggs. Beat the eggs at low speed for 1 minute or until thoroughly mixed. Add the salt and milk and continue to beat. While still beating, add the melted, cooled butter, a little at a time.

Lightly butter the bottom and sides of a double boiler top and place over just barely simmering water. Pour in the egg mixture, cover and allow to cook at low temperature for 10 minutes.

After the 10 minutes are up, turn the congealed portion of the eggs to the middle of the pan; cover and continue to cook for 5 minutes longer or until all of the eggs are in large congealed pieces. Serve on a heated platter. Serves 4.

This is also a good way to scramble eggs for a crowd, if you have a large double boiler. The eggs stay tender and have a wonderful flavor. The eggs can also be kept warm over hot water without losing any of their eye or taste appeal.

Chapter VI

OMELETS—FRENCH, AMERICAN AND SPANISH

THE ARGUMENT OVER how to make a good omelet has been raging between cooks for centuries. There are as many schools of omelet preparation as there are nations. Notable among these are the French, American and Spanish styles.

The French style of omelet is made by beating the yolks and whites together. The egg mixture and its various added tidbits of flavor is then poured into a hot enamel or iron skillet which has a layer of sizzling butter covering the bottom.

The French omelet is usually completely cooked on the top of the stove. As the omelet thickens and congeals, the edges are lifted with a spatula and tilted slightly to allow the undone portion to run back into the hot skillet. This is continued until the whole omelet is cooked. When completely cooked, the top of a French omelet somewhat resembles moist scrambled eggs. The omelet is then folded in half and served.

The American style of omelet greatly resembles a soufflé. The yolks and whites are beaten separately, and then the stiff and puffy whites are folded into the yolk mixture. The omelet is then placed in a hot, oven-proof skillet which is coated with melted butter.

The American omelet is first cooked on top of the stove. When the bottom of the omelet has cooked to a delicate, golden brown, the whole omelet, pan and all, is transferred to the top rack of a moderate oven and baked until the top is puffy and golden.

The Spanish style of omelet is made by beating the eggs until they are well mixed and slightly bubbly; various tidbits of meat, vegetables etc. are added. It is then fried in olive oil or butter like a huge pancake. When the bottom is a golden brown, the whole omelet is turned over and the cooking is completed on top of the stove. Spanish omelets are usually served flat, topped by a flavorful sauce.

Whether your preference leans to the French, American

or Spanish omelet, it is important to remember that a good omelet cannot be rushed into deliciousness by high temperatures and rapid cooking. Low temperatures and patience give the best results.

All omelets should be served on a heated plate or platter. If the omelet is transferred to a cold plate, the bottom will become tough and unpalatable.

BASIC FRENCH OMELET

6 eggs
½ cup milk
½ teaspoon salt
⅛ teaspoon pepper
2 tablespoons butter

Beat the eggs just enough to blend the yolks and whites together well. Stir in the milk, salt and pepper.

Melt the butter in a heavy skillet over low heat. When it is completely melted and just beginning to bubble, pour in the egg mixture. Cook for 1 minute or until the edges begin to get firm. With a spatula or pancake turner, lift the edges and permit the uncooked egg mixture to run into the bottom of the pan. When the eggs are an even, creamy consistency, increase the heat so that the bottom is browned slightly. Fold the omelet in half and serve. Serves 4.

Variations:

Chive Omelet: When the omelet is creamy and just before folding, sprinkle two tablespoons of chives, finely chopped, over the surface and then fold in half.

Chicken Omelet: Heat ¾ cup chicken meat, finely chopped, in a small amount of butter and add to the omelet just before folding.

Ham Omelet: Heat ¾ cup of lean, chopped ham in a skillet over low heat and add to the omelet just before folding.

Cheese Omelet: When the omelet is of even and creamy consistency, sprinkle the surface with ¾ cup grated Cheddar or mild American cheese and then fold in half and serve.

Jelly Omelet: Break up ½ cup currant or any jelly with a fork and drizzle over the omelet just before folding in half.

SWEETBREAD SPANISH OMELET

6 sweetbreads
½ teaspoon salt
¼ cup butter
1 cup onion, coarsely chopped
½ cup cooking sherry or white wine
1 cup canned tomatoes
1 tablespoon minced parsley
2 (additional) tablespoons butter
6 eggs
½ cup boiled ham, finely chopped

Soak the sweetbreads in cold water for 1 hour. Change the water three times during the soaking or put them under very slowly running cold water for 1 hour. Place the sweetbreads in a saucepan with cold water to cover; add the salt and bring to a rolling boil for 5 minutes. After cooking, rinse thoroughly under cold running water. Drain; remove and discard any thick tissue. Cut up into ½-inch cubes; press dry between sheets of paper toweling until all the moisture is removed.

Melt the ¼ cup butter in a skillet with a tightly fitting cover. Add the chopped onion and sauté until it begins to get limp and transparent. Add the sweetbreads and continue to sauté until they begin to turn a golden brown around the edges. Add the wine, tomatoes and parsley. Turn the heat back to simmer, cover and continue to simmer for 30 minutes, stirring occasionally.

Place the additional two tablespoons of butter in a skillet over moderate heat. When the butter has melted, beat the eggs until they are mixed and slightly bubbly. Stir in the boiled ham. Pour the ham and egg mixture into the melted butter and cook until the bottom side is a light golden brown. Using a broad spatula, turn the whole omelet over and cook the other side until a golden brown.

Place the omelet on a heated platter and pour the sweetbread sauce over the top and around the edges. Serve at once. Serves 6.

CHEESE AND TOMATO OMELET

Omelet:
6 eggs, separated
2 tablespoons milk
½ teaspoon salt
¼ teaspoon pepper
2 tablespoons butter

Topping:
1 #2 can stewed tomatoes (most supermarkets carry these
   tomatoes already stewed with green pepper, etc.)
1 tablespoon butter
½ teaspoon salt
⅛ teaspoon pepper
1 teaspoon granulated sugar
1 cup grated American cheese

Beat the egg yolks until they are light and lemon colored;
add the milk, salt and pepper. Mix well. Beat the egg whites
until they stand in stiff peaks. Fold the beaten whites into the
egg yolk mixture. Melt the butter in a 10-inch skillet over
moderate heat; swirl the butter around so that it covers the
sides of the pan as well as the bottom. Pour in the egg mixture
and continue to cook over moderate heat for 7 minutes or
until the omelet has set.

Place the tomatoes, butter, salt, pepper and sugar in a saucepan and place over moderate heat. Cook for 10 minutes or
until slightly thickened.

Using a spatula, lift the omelet around the edges from time
to time to loosen it from the bottom of the pan. When the
bottom of the omelet is a golden brown, place half the tomatoes
over the surface. Follow this with all the grated cheese. Place
the omelet, still in the skillet, in a 350° F. oven for about 10
minutes or until the cheese has melted.

Remove the omelet from the oven and fold in half. Slide
the folded omelet on to a heated serving platter and drizzle
the remainder of the tomatoes over the top for garnish.

Serve piping hot. Serves 6.

⅓ cup butter
⅓ cup flour
1½ cups milk
½ teaspoon salt
½ teaspoon Accent
2 7½-ounce cans tiny shrimp, drained
6 eggs, separated
¼ (additional) cup butter
2 tablespoons parsley, finely chopped

Melt the ⅓ cup butter in the top of a double boiler; stir in the flour until it is smoothly blended. Add the milk, salt and Accent and place over boiling water. Cook, stirring constantly, until the mixture has thickened. Remove ⅔ cup of the thickened sauce and set aside to cool to room temperature. Add the drained shrimp to the remainder of the cream sauce in the double boiler. Cover and turn the heat back to barely simmering.

Beat the egg yolks until light colored and slightly thickened; add the cooled white sauce and beat again to mix thoroughly.

Beat the egg whites until they are stiff and stand in peaks. Fold the beaten egg whites into the yolk-cream sauce mixture.

Melt the additional butter in a 10-inch skillet with a fitted cover. Pour the egg mixture into the skillet. Smooth the top slightly with a rubber spoon. Lightly butter the skillet's cover and place over the omelet. Cook on top of the stove over low heat for 15 minutes or until the sides and the bottom of the omelet have turned a light golden brown and the omelet is puffed up and cooked through.

Cut through the center with a sharp knife to within ½ inch of the bottom. Loosen the omelet and transfer to a heated platter. Pour the heated shrimp mixture over half the omelet and then fold the other half over the top of the shrimp. Garnish the top with a sprinkle of parsley. Serve at once. Serves 4.

CRISP BACON OMELET, AMERICAN STYLE

8 strips lean bacon, about 10 inches long and ⅛ inch thick
6 eggs, separated
3 tablespoons tepid water
½ teaspoon salt
¼ teaspoon freshly ground pepper
⅓ cup butter
2 tablespoons parsley, finely chopped

Cut the bacon up into ½-inch squares. Place in a skillet over moderate heat and sauté until crisp and golden. Drain the bacon squares on paper toweling and set aside until later.

Beat the egg whites until they just begin to get frothy; add the water and continue to beat until they are stiff and stand in shiny peaks. Beat the egg yolks until they are light and slightly thickened; add the salt and pepper and mix well.

Fold in the egg whites lightly. Be sure they are evenly distributed in the yolks. Turn the oven to 325° F. and allow to preheat.

Melt the butter in a large, oven-proof skillet over moderate heat on top of the stove. Pour in the egg mixture. Cook over low heat on top of the stove for about 20 minutes or until the bottom edge appears a golden brown when lifted with the blade of a knife. Do not stir or disturb the center of the omelet while it is cooking.

Then, carefully place the omelet, skillet and all, into the preheated 325° F. oven for an additional 5 to 8 minutes of cooking; the top should become slightly dry and just lightly tanned.

Remove the omelet from the oven; sprinkle the crisp bacon squares over ½ the omelet. Using a very sharp knife, cut through the middle; using a broad spatula fold in half, enclosing the bacon. Again using the broad spatula, remove the omelet to a heated platter. Sprinkle the parsley over the top of the folded omelet and serve. Serves 4.

RUM DESSERT OMELET

6 eggs, separated
1 tablespoon light brown sugar
2 tablespoons granulated sugar
½ teaspoon rum extract flavoring
⅛ teaspoon salt
2 tablespoons butter
¼ cup rum

Beat the egg yolks until they are light and lemon colored. Add the brown sugar, granulated sugar, rum flavoring and salt. Beat again for a few seconds until thoroughly mixed. Set aside.

Beat the egg whites until they stand in peaks. Carefully fold the egg whites into the yolk mixture. Take care to retain all the air.

Melt the butter in a skillet and pour the mixture into the melted butter. Cook over low heat until the edges begin to get firm. Using a spatula, lift up the edges of the omelet, allowing the uncooked portion to run underneath. As soon as all of the liquid portion is cooked, fold in half and transfer to a warm, oven-proof platter. Pour the rum over the top of the omelet and ignite. Bring the omelet to the table while still blazing. Serves 6.

Note: In choosing the rum for pouring over desserts of this type, always check the alcoholic content on the bottle; if the rum is 80 proof or less, you will have difficulty in lighting it. If you cannot find high-proof rum, use 100 proof grain alcohol flavored with a few drops of rum flavoring.

CORN OMELET

6 eggs, separated
3 tablespoons water at room temperature
½ teaspoon salt
1 12-ounce can niblet corn with pimiento, drained very dry
¼ cup butter

Beat the egg yolks until light colored and slightly thickened. Set aside. Beat the egg whites until they begin to get frothy; add the water and salt and continue to beat until they stand in shiny peaks.

Alternately fold in the egg whites and the niblet corn into the yolk mixture. Preheat oven to 325° F.

Melt the butter in an oven-proof skillet over moderate heat. Pour in the egg mixture and cook over low heat until the bottom is a light, golden brown. Lift the edge of the omelet with a table knife to see if it is properly browned.

Place the omelet in the preheated 325° F. oven for 8 minutes or until the top is a very light golden brown. Cut the omelet in half, fold over, slide on to a heated platter and serve at once. Serves 4 generously.

If you desire, additional butter can be inserted in between the halves of the omelet just before serving.

SPANISH OMELET

Spanish omelets differ from French omelets in that they are served flat and not folded over. Here is a delightful omelet that utilizes left-over potatoes.

½ cup onion, diced in ¼-inch cubes
2 tablespoons olive oil or butter
2 cups boiled potatoes, diced in ½-inch cubes
½ teaspoon salt
¼ teaspoon freshly ground pepper
6 eggs
1 teaspoon water

Place the onion and the olive oil in a skillet over moderate heat. Sauté until the onion begins to get limp and transparent. Add the diced potatoes and continue to sauté until the edges just begin to turn a golden brown. Sprinkle the salt and pepper over the top.

Beat the eggs until they are thoroughly mixed and slightly bubbly. Add the teaspoon of water and beat again for a second or so. Pour the beaten eggs over the potatoes and onions. Cover and cook for 5 minutes or until the edges of the eggs begin to turn a golden brown. Using a broad spatula, turn the whole omelet over and cook the other side until a golden brown. Add a little more oil or butter if needed. Serve at once. Serves 4 generously.

MUSHROOM OMELET, FRENCH STYLE

2 cups sliced fresh mushrooms
¼ cup butter
6 eggs
1 teaspoon salt
⅛ teaspoon freshly ground pepper
⅓ cup milk
¼ (additional) cup butter
1 10-ounce can cream of mushroom soup

Sauté the mushrooms in ¼ cup butter until they are heated through and just beginning to turn golden brown on the edges. Divide the mushrooms in half and allow one half of the mixture to cool in a separate bowl. Turn the heat to barely simmering under the remainder of the mushrooms.

Beat the eggs with a fork or rotary beater until they are mixed. Add the salt, pepper and milk and beat again for a second or so. Stir in the cooled portion of the mushrooms.

Melt the additional ¼ cup butter in another skillet over moderate heat. Add the egg-mushroom mixture; turn the heat back to very low and cook for 7 to 10 minutes. Using a fork, lift the edges of the omelet during the cooking time and allow the undone portion to run back into the skillet.

Add the mushroom soup just as it comes from the can to the remainder of the sautéed mushrooms. Stir well and allow to heat through.

When the center of the omelet is firm to the touch, cut in half and slide on to a heated platter. Pour the mushrooms and the soup over half of the omelet and fold the other half over the top. Serve at once, piping hot. Serves 4.

FINES HERBES OMELET

6 eggs
2 tablespoons butter
1 tablespoon parsley, finely chopped
1 tablespoon chives, finely chopped
½ teaspoon salt
⅛ teaspoon black pepper
1 brimming teaspoon water

Beat the eggs until they are light and bubbly; set aside.

Melt the butter over low heat in a skillet. Mix the chopped parsley and the chopped chives with the eggs. Add the salt and pepper and water and mix again.

Pour the egg mixture in the skillet and cook over low heat until the omelet begins to set. Using a spatula, lift the omelet at the edges and let the undone portion run underneath until all is evenly cooked. Fold in half and serve at once, piping hot. Serves 6, allowing 1 egg per person. If you want more generous portions, double or triple the recipe.

ORIENTAL OMELETS

1 2-ounce envelope dehydrated chicken noodle soup mix
½ cup warm water
½ cup celery, diced in ¼-inch cubes
1 7½-ounce can shrimp bits and pieces, drained, or ¾ cup cooked, deveined, chopped shrimp
½ cup scallion, sliced paper thin; include a little of the green
6 eggs
1 teaspoon soy sauce
½ cup peanut oil

Place the dehydrated soup mix in the warm water in a saucepan over low heat. Bring to a slow boil and then cook for 2 minutes, stirring frequently. Remove from the heat and allow to cool to room temperature.

Mix the celery, shrimp and sliced scallions together lightly. Beat the eggs until they are thoroughly mixed and add the soy sauce. Beat for 1 second longer to mix. Add the celery and shrimp mixture; then add the cooled soup mixture. Mix all well.

Heat a portion of the oil on a griddle or in a large skillet. Using a quarter cup measure, place ¼ cup of the egg mixture into the hot oil and sauté until the underside is a delicate golden brown. Turn over and brown the other side. Drain the little omelets on paper toweling and serve. Makes 8 omelets. Serves 4, allowing 2 omelets per person.

SPANISH OMELET DINNER

8 eggs
1 4-ounce can mushroom stems and pieces, drained and coarsely chopped
1 7-ounce can shrimp bits and pieces, drained and coarsely chopped
1 cup boiled potatoes, coarsely chopped
1 4-ounce can peas and carrots, drained
¼ cup onion, finely chopped
1 cup chili sauce
Salt and pepper to taste
½ cup butter

A 6-inch skillet with a rounded bottom is ideal for this omelet dinner because you can make 4 uniform omelets and then stack them one on top of another.

For the first omelet, beat two eggs until light and fluffy. Add the drained mushrooms and mix well. Using 2 tablespoons of butter, sauté in a flat omelet much like a large pancake. When both sides have browned, place on an oven-proof dish in a warm oven. Mix the chili sauce, onion and a dash of salt and pepper together. Place ¼ cup of the chili sauce mixture over the omelet. Reserve the rest.

Proceed to the second omelet, again using 2 well-beaten eggs and add the shrimp pieces. When sautéed, place this omelet on top of the first one; again top with ¼ cup of the reserved chili sauce mixture.

Make the third omelet with the potatoes and the fourth omelet with the drained peas and carrots. As the omelets are finished top each with the onion-flavored chili sauce, ending up with chili sauce on top of the stack of four omelets. Remove from the oven and cut into wedges as you would a cake. Serve piping hot. Serves 6.

Chapter VII

SOUFFLÉ SECRETS

THE FRENCH WORD for a light, airy dish is "soufflé". This is, the most adequate description one can find for a properly made, delicious soufflé. Eggs perform the magic alchemy needed to make a soufflé light and airy.

Soufflés fall into two catagories. They can be made with hearty ingredients such as meat, fish, fowl or vegetables and can be served as a main dish for dinner or luncheon. Soufflés can also be made with flavorings of fruit, jams and liquors; these are called dessert soufflés.

A soufflé must be served almost immediately after it is made. Most soufflés will start to fall as they cool. It is better to have everyone seated and waiting at the table when soufflé is the fare. If your guests dawdle and are not prompt, your soufflé will suffer and all of your efforts and materials will have been in vain.

Dessert soufflés should be started baking when your guests are about midway through the main part of the meal. In this way, the soufflé will have reached its peak of perfection right about the time your guests are ready for it.

Soufflés, for the most part, are most successful when baked in an ungreased casserole or baking dish. As the soufflé rises during baking, it clings to the sides of the ungreased dish and is able to climb to high and puffy heights. If the dish is greased, the soufflé loses its grip on the side walls and falls flat.

ORANGE DESSERT SOUFFLÉ

Soufflé:
⅓ cup soft butter
⅓ cup all-purpose flour
⅛ teaspoon salt
1 cup milk
½ cup thawed frozen orange juice concentrate
6 eggs, separated
¼ cup granulated sugar

Topping:
1 8-ounce can mandarin oranges
½ cup granulated sugar
2 tablespoons cornstarch
½ cup thawed frozen orange juice concentrate

Melt the butter in a saucepan; stir in the flour and salt and cook until the mixture begins to bubble. Add the milk and cook over low heat, stirring constantly, until the mixture is thick. Remove from the heat and add the thawed orange juice concentrate. Mix well and set aside to cool slightly.

Beat the egg yolks until they are thick and lemon colored; add 3 tablespoons of the orange-flavored mixture and mix well. Then add the egg yolks to the orange mixture and stir until thoroughly mixed.

Beat the egg whites until they just begin to stand in peaks; gradually add the sugar and continue to beat until they stand in glossy peaks. Carefully fold the egg whites into the yolk-orange mixture. Pour into a suitable unbuttered casserole dish. Bake in a 300° F. oven for 1¼ hours or until a table knife inserted in the middle comes out clean.

For the topping, drain the mandarin oranges, reserving the juice. Add enough water to the juice to make 1 cup. Mix the sugar and cornstarch together thoroughly; stir into the juice and water and mix until smooth. Place in a saucepan over low heat and add the thawed orange juice concentrate. Cook over low heat, stirring constantly, until the mixture becomes thickened. Remove from heat and stir in the mandarin orange sections. Take care not to break up the orange sections. Serve warm over portions of the soufflé. Serves 6.

MACARONI SOUFFLÉ WITH CREAMED TUNA

1 6-ounce package elbow macaroni
¼ cup butter
¼ cup flour
1 teaspoon salt
⅛ teaspoon pepper
1¼ cups milk
5 eggs, separated
2 10-ounce cans cream of chicken soup
2 7½-ounce cans light meat tuna fish, drained well

Boil the macaroni until tender according to package directions. Drain and set aside.

Melt the butter in a saucepan over moderate heat. Stir in the flour, salt and pepper and mix until smooth and free of lumps. Add the milk and continue to cook over moderate heat, stirring constantly, until the sauce is thickened and creamy. Remove from the heat and allow to cool to room temperature.

Beat the egg yolks until light and slightly thickened. Beat ½ cup of the thickened, cooled cream sauce into the egg yolks; then add the remainder of the cream sauce to the yolks, beating until all is well mixed.

Stir the drained macaroni into the egg yolk mixture and mix well.

Beat the egg whites until they stand in peaks and are shiny, but not dry. Gently fold the egg whites into the macaroni and egg yolk mixture.

Line a well-greased ring mold with white bakery paper cut to fit the sides, bottom and the ring opening. The paper may overlap if necessary to cover all of the metal of the ring mold. Butter the paper lining with a little melted butter and a pastry brush. Using a rubber spoon, carefully place the egg and macaroni mixture around the sides of the mold. Place in a 325° F. oven for 45 minutes or until a table knife inserted into the middle of the mixture comes out clean.

While the ring is baking, place the two cans of cream of chicken soup over barely boiling water in the top of a double boiler. Flake the drained tuna fish and add to the cream of chicken soup. Cover and allow to heat through.

When the macaroni-soufflé ring is done, unmold on a heated platter and pour the creamed tuna mixture into the middle. Serve at once, piping hot. Serves 6.

BEEF SOUFFLÉ

¼ cup butter
¼ cup all-purpose flour
1 cup milk
5 eggs, separated
1 cup boiling water
1 4-ounce jar dried beef
⅛ teaspoon freshly ground pepper

Melt the butter in a saucepan over moderate heat. Stir in the flour and mix until you have a smooth paste. Add the milk and continue to cook over moderate heat, stirring constantly, until the mixture is thick and creamy. Remove from the heat and allow to cool slightly.

Beat the egg yolks until they are light and slightly thickened. Add ¼ cup of the cream sauce to the beaten yolks and beat again. Continue to beat and add the rest of the cream sauce gradually.

Pour the boiling water over the dried beef and let stand for 1 minute; then drain. Using a kitchen shears, snip the dried beef up into ⅛-inch strips. Add the snipped beef to the yolk-cream sauce mixture, mixing all very well.

Beat the egg whites until they are stiff and shiny, but not dry. Fold the beaten egg whites into the beef mixture gently. Using a rubber spoon, place the mixture in a 1½-quart ungreased casserole.

Bake in a 325° F. oven for 55 minutes or until the top is a rich, golden brown. Serve at once. Serves 4.

SIMPLE EGG SOUFFLÉ

1 tablespoon butter
1 tablespoon all-purpose flour
1 cup milk
6 eggs, separated
½ teaspoon salt

Melt the butter in a saucepan and stir in the flour. When the mixture is smooth and slightly bubbly, add the milk and continue to cook, stirring constantly, until the mixture has thickened. Remove from the heat and allow to cool to room temperature.

Beat the egg yolks until they are light and lemon colored; add the salt; mix well and add to the cooled cream sauce. Beat together until thoroughly mixed.

Beat the egg whites until they stand in peaks. Gently fold the egg whites into the cream sauce and egg mixture. Pour into a 1-quart, ungreased casserole. Place in a 325° F. oven for 10 minutes. Raise the heat to 350° F. and bake for an additional 15 minutes or until the soufflé is a golden brown and highly puffed up. Serve piping hot. Serves 6.

CHEESE SOUFFLÉ

¼ cup butter
¼ cup flour
¼ teaspoon salt
1 cup milk
1 cup shredded Cheddar cheese
4 eggs, separated
1 teaspoon powdered mustard
Dash of cayenne pepper
¼ teaspoon freshly ground pepper
¼ teaspoon cream of tartar

Melt the butter in a saucepan over low heat; stir in the flour and salt and continue to cook over low heat until the mixture bubbles. Add the milk slowly and continue to cook over low heat, stirring constantly, until the mixture has thickened and coats the spoon. Add the shredded cheese and continue to cook and stir until the cheese has completely melted. Remove from heat.

Beat the egg yolks until they are lemon colored. Stir 2 tablespoons of the hot cheese sauce into the egg yolks and then add the yolks to the cheese sauce, mixing thoroughly. Add the powdered mustard, cayenne pepper and mix again.

Beat the egg whites until they begin to get bubbly; add the cream of tartar and continue to beat until they stand in stiff peaks. Gently fold the beaten whites into the cheese mixture, taking care not to lose the air.

Pour the mixture into an ungreased 1½-quart casserole dish. Place the dish in a pan of water in a 350° F. oven for 1 hour or until the soufflé is puffed up and golden brown. Serve at once, piping hot. Serves 6.

ORANGE MARMALADE SOUFFLÉ

1 cup orange marmalade that is heavy with orange peel and
   light on the jelly content
6 eggs, separated
¾ cup powdered sugar
1 teaspoon vanilla
¼ cup good grape brandy
1½ cups chilled whipping cream

Butter the top half of a large double boiler which has a
tightly fitting cover. Set aside. Have the water in the bottom
half of the boiler at a slow boiling point before you start the
soufflé.

Beat the egg whites until they are stiff and stand in shiny
peaks. Gently fold the cup of marmalade, a little at a time, into
the egg whites. The marmalade should be evenly distributed.
Place the mixture in the buttered top of the double boiler. It
should come to a little over half full. Cover tightly and place
over the slowly boiling water. Cook over the boiling water for
1 hour. Have additional boiling water ready to add to the
bottom of the boiler should it become too low. Do not open up
or remove the cover during this hour's cooking time.

Beat the egg yolks until they are thick and lemon colored.
Gradually add the powdered sugar, vanilla and brandy. Continue to beat until all is mixed. Beat the whipping cream until
it stands in peaks. Fold the whipped cream into the egg yolk
mixture and place in the refrigerator to cool until the marmalade portion is cooked.

Serve the chilled sauce over the hot pudding. Serves 6.

This is a most flexible party dessert, for the marmalade
portion can be left standing over hot water after it has cooked.

CHICKEN SOUFFLÉ SUPREME

¼ cup butter
¼ cup flour
¼ teaspoon salt
⅛ teaspoon pepper
1 cup milk
4 eggs, separated
1 cup chicken, finely chopped; use both white and dark meat

Melt the butter in a saucepan over moderate heat. Stir in the
flour, salt and pepper. Mix until a smooth paste is formed.

Add the milk and continue to cook and stir until thickened and smooth. Remove from the heat and allow to cool.

Beat the egg yolks until they are light and frothy. Add a small portion of the white sauce and continue beating. Continue beating until all the white sauce has been added. Fold in the chopped chicken.

Beat the egg whites until they stand in peaks and are shiny but not dry. Gently fold the beaten egg whites into the yolk and chicken mixture.

Using a rubber spoon, place the mixture into an ungreased 1½-quart casserole. Bake in a 325° F. oven for 1 hour or until the surface of the soufflé is a rich golden brown. Serve immediately. Serves 4.

SALMON SOUFFLÉ

4 eggs, separated
1 1-pound can pink salmon, drained
½ teaspoon salt
¼ teaspoon pepper
¼ teaspoon paprika
2 tablespoons cider vinegar
2 tablespoons lemon juice
½ cup fine cracker crumbs
½ cup scalding hot milk

Place the egg yolks in a mixing bowl and beat until they are light and bubbly.

Remove all the bones and skin from the salmon and discard. Add the salmon to the beaten yolks. Add the salt, pepper, paprika, vinegar and lemon juice. Mix all well, breaking up the salmon into small flakes. Add the cracker crumbs and mix thoroughly; add the hot milk and mix again.

Beat the egg whites until they are stiff and stand in peaks. Gently fold the beaten egg whites into the salmon mixture, taking care not to lose the air.

Place in a 1½-quart ungreased casserole; gently smooth the top with a rubber spoon. Bake in a 350° F. oven for 55 minutes or until a table knife inserted in the center comes out clean. Serve at once, serve piping hot. Serves 6.

MACAROON SOUFFLÉ

1 dozen 2-inch diameter macaroons
1 cup milk
4 eggs, separated
1 6-ounce package frozen sugared strawberries, slightly thawed
1 cup chilled whipping cream

Crush the macaroons until they are the consistency of coarse corn meal. Scald the milk in the top of a double boiler over rapidly boiling water. Stir the macaroon crumbs into the scalded milk.

Beat the egg yolks until they are thick and lemon colored. Add 3 tablespoons of the hot milk mixture to the beaten yolks. Mix well and then add the yolks to the hot milk mixture. Continue to cook over slowly boiling water, stirring constantly, until the mixture thickens and coats the spoon. Remove from the heat and allow to cool for 5 minutes.

Beat the egg whites until they are stiff and stand in peaks. Fold the egg whites into the milk-macaroon mixture. Pour into an unbuttered 1½-quart casserole or mold. Place in a pan of water and bake in a 350° F. oven for 25 minutes or until puffed up and golden brown.

Using a sharp knife, loosen the soufflé around the edges and unmold on to a platter. Chop the strawberries coarsely and drizzle them over the top of the soufflé. Whip the cream until it stands in peaks. Place the whipped cream around the outer edge of the soufflé. Serves 6.

POTATO SOUFFLÉ

2 cups instant mashed potatoes, cooked according to package directions
4 slices lean boiled ham, 6 x 4 x 1/16 inch thick
6 eggs, separated
½ teaspoon salt
¼ teaspoon pepper

Place the mashed potatoes in a mixing bowl and allow to cool slightly.

Cut the ham up into pieces 2 inches long x ¼ inch wide. Mix with the warm potatoes.

Beat the egg yolks with a whisk or rotary beater until they

are thoroughly mixed and bubbly. Add the beaten yolks, salt and pepper to the potato mixture and beat until light and fluffy and thoroughly mixed.

Beat the egg whites until they are stiff and stand in firm peaks. Gently fold the beaten whites into the potato mixture.

Place in a 1½-quart ungreased casserole and bake at 325° F. for 25 minutes or until puffed up and a delicate golden brown. Serve at once, piping hot. Serves 6.

CHEESE AND CHIVE SOUFFLÉ

¼ cup butter
¼ cup all-purpose flour
¾ cup milk
½ teaspoon salt
1 cup grated Cheddar cheese or sharp American cheese
4 eggs, separated
1 tablespoon chopped chives

Melt the butter in a saucepan; stir in the flour and continue to cook over low heat until the mixture begins to bubble. Gradually add the milk. Cook, stirring constantly, over low heat until the mixture has thickened. Add the salt and grated cheese and continue to cook over very low heat, stirring constantly, until the cheese has completely melted. Remove from the heat and allow the mixture to cool to room temperature.

Beat the egg yolks until they are light and lemon colored. Mix the egg yolks into the cheese mixture; add the chopped chives and mix thoroughly.

Beat the egg whites until they stand in peaks. Fold the egg whites into the cheese mixture, taking care to retain the air. Pour the mixture into a suitable ungreased baking dish. Place the baking dish in a pan of hot water and bake in a 350° F. oven for 40 minutes or until puffed up and golden brown. Serve at once. Serves 6.

BLEACHED CELERY SOUFFLÉ

¼ cup butter
1 cup bleached celery, cut up in ¼-inch cubes; include a few
    tender leaves
¼ cup all-purpose flour
1 cup half-and-half cream
½ teaspoon salt
⅛ teaspoon freshly ground pepper
5 eggs, separated

Melt the butter in a saucepan over moderate heat. Add the
chopped celery and cook for 5 minutes. Stir in the flour and
mix well. Add the half-and-half cream and continue to cook
over moderate heat, stirring constantly, until the mixture is
thickened. Add the salt and pepper; mix well and set aside
to cool slightly.

Beat the egg yolks until they are light and slightly thickened.
Add ¼ cup of the celery mixture to the eggs and continue to
beat for a second or two longer; then add the yolk mixture to
the celery mixture and mix well. Set aside.

Beat the egg whites until they are stiff and shiny but not
dry. Fold the beaten egg whites into the yolk-celery mixture.

Using a rubber spoon, place in an ungreased 1½-quart casserole. Bake in a 325° F. oven for 50 minutes or until the top
is a rich golden brown. Serve immediately. Serves 4.

SPINACH SOUFFLÉ

2 tablespoons butter
1 tablespoon green onion, finely chopped
2 tablespoons all-purpose flour
1 cup milk
2 10-ounce packages frozen, chopped spinach
2 tablespoons grated Cheddar or mild American cheese
4 eggs, separated
½ teaspoon salt
⅛ teaspoon black pepper

Melt the butter in a large skillet. Add the onion and sauté
until limp and transparent. Stir in the flour; when the mixture
begins to bubble, gradually add the milk. Cook over moderate
heat, stirring constantly, until the mixture begins to thicken.
Add the chopped spinach and continue to cook until the spin-

ach is tender, stirring constantly. Remove from the heat and allow to cool. When cool, stir in the grated cheese.

Beat the egg yolks until they are thoroughly mixed and add them along with the salt and pepper to the spinach mixture. Mix thoroughly.

Beat the egg whites until they stand in peaks. Fold the beaten egg whites into the spinach mixture taking care not to lose the air. Pour into a 1-quart casserole dish. Place the dish in a pan of water in a 350° F. oven and bake for ½ hour or until the mixture rises and is firmly set. Serves 6.

CHOCOLATE SOUFFLÉ

2 tablespoons butter
2 tablespoons all-purpose flour
¾ cup milk
1 2-ounce square semi-sweet baking chocolate
1½ cups granulated sugar
2 tablespoons hot water
4 eggs, separated
1 teaspoon vanilla

Melt the butter in a saucepan and stir in the flour. When the mixture just begins to bubble, gradually add the milk. Continue to cook over low heat, stirring constantly, until the mixture comes to the boiling point and is slightly thickened. Remove from the heat and set aside.

Grate the chocolate and add to the milk mixture. Gradually add the sugar. Stir after each addition. Add the hot water and mix well.

Beat the egg yolks until they are lemon colored. Take 3 tablespoons of the chocolate mixture and add to the egg yolks, then add the egg yolks to the chocolate mixture. Mix thoroughly. Allow to cool slightly, add the vanilla and mix again.

Beat the egg whites until they stand in firm peaks. Fold the beaten whites into the chocolate mixture taking care not to lose any of the air. Pour into an unbuttered casserole dish and place the casserole in a pan of water. Bake in a 350° F. oven for 25 minutes or until puffed up and firmly set. Serves 6.

CHILLED COFFEE SOUFFLÉ

1 tablespoon unflavored gelatin
½ cup cold milk
1½ cups fairly strong coffee
⅔ cup granulated sugar
⅛ teaspoon salt
3 eggs, separated
1 teaspoon vanilla

Place the unflavored gelatin in the cold milk to soften for about 5 minutes.

Place the coffee, sugar and salt in the top of a double boiler. Mix well. Add the gelatin and milk and mix again. Place over slowly boiling water and cook until the mixture is steaming hot, stirring frequently.

Beat the egg yolks until they are light and lemon colored. Add 3 tablespoons of the hot, coffee-flavored mixture to the beaten yolks; mix well, and then add the yolks to the coffee-flavored mixture in the double boiler. Mix thoroughly and continue to cook, stirring constantly, until the mixture coats the spoon. Remove from the heat and allow to cool for 5 minutes. Add the vanilla.

Beat the egg whites until they are stiff and stand in peaks. Fold the egg whites into the coffee-flavored mixture. Take great care to retain all of the air in the egg whites. Pour into a mold and chill in the refrigerator at least 4 hours. Serves 6.

TUNA FISH SOUFFLÉ

¼ cup butter or margarine
1 tablespoon scallion, finely chopped
¼ cup all-purpose flour
1 cup milk
5 eggs, separated
1 7½-ounce can light tuna fish, drained well
¼ cup parsley, finely chopped
⅛ teaspoon freshly ground pepper

Melt the butter in a saucepan over moderate heat. Add the chopped scallion and cook until limp and transparent. Stir in the flour and mix until smooth and free of lumps. Add the milk and continue to cook, stirring constantly, until the mixture has become thick and creamy. Remove from the heat and allow to cool slightly.

Beat the egg yolks until light and thick. Add a small portion of the cream sauce and continue to beat; then stir the yolks into the cream sauce.

Flake the tuna fish and add to the cream sauce, along with the parsley and pepper. Mix all very well.

Beat the egg whites until they stand in peaks and are shiny but not dry. Gently fold the egg whites into the tuna mixture.

Using a rubber spoon, place the mixture in an ungreased 1½-quart casserole. Bake in a 325° F. oven for 55 minutes or until the top is a rich, golden brown. Serve at once. Serves 4.

Chapter VIII

EGG CUSTARDS AND PUDDINGS

MENTION "EGG CUSTARD" to most people and they immediately envision some poor bedridden soul too weak to take solid foods. It is too bad this delicious dessert had to be relegated to sick bay. Egg custards are not only delicious; they are loaded with good nourishment, easy to digest, protein rich and light enough to follow almost any type of meal you are serving.

Home-made puddings, too, have fallen into obscurity. Granted, all of those wonderful puddings which come in packages and can be whipped up in seconds flat have their place in today's fast pace. But when you have the time and ingredients, try making your own egg-rich puddings. The difference in taste and family praise will be immediately noted.

BAKED EGG CUSTARD

4 cups milk
6 eggs, separated
½ cup granulated sugar
1 teaspoon vanilla

Place the milk in a double boiler over rapidly boiling water and heat to just below the scalding point.

Place the egg yolks in a bowl along with the sugar and mix the two thoroughly. Add the hot milk a little at a time, beating slowly after each addition.

Beat the egg whites until they just begin to stand in peaks. Add the vanilla and beat for 1 second longer. Fold the egg whites into the yolk mixture.

Pour the custard into a lightly buttered 2-quart casserole. Place the casserole dish in a pan of water and bake at 325° F for ½ hour or until a knife inserted in the middle comes out clean. Serves 6. This custard is delicious served either hot or cold.

CARAMEL COATED CUSTARD

¼ cup granulated sugar
¼ cup water
4 egg yolks (see Chapter XIII for using left-over whites)
2 tablespoons light brown sugar
2 cups milk
1 teaspoon vanilla

Mix the granulated sugar and water together in a saucepan and cook, stirring frequently, over moderate heat until it caramelizes (356° F. on a candy thermometer). Pour the caramel into a lightly buttered mold and set aside.

Beat the egg yolks until they are light and lemon colored. Add the brown sugar and beat until the sugar is thoroughly mixed.

Heat the milk to just below the scalding point. Add several spoonfuls of the hot milk to the egg yolks, beat well and then gradually add the egg yolks to the hot milk, beating constantly. Add the vanilla and mix well. Allow to cool slightly.

By this time, the caramel should be slightly set and skinned over in the waiting mold. Gently pour in the egg yolk and milk mixture. Place the mold in a pan of water and bake at 325° F. for 25 minutes or until the center is set. Turn out on a serving dish. The caramel will run down the sides and glaze the custard. Serves 6.

EASY BAKED CUSTARD

4 eggs
½ cup granulated sugar
¼ teaspoon salt
2 teaspoons vanilla
2 cups evaporated milk
1¼ cups tepid water

Beat the eggs until they are thoroughly mixed and are beginning to get bubbly. Add the sugar, salt and vanilla. Beat again until the sugar is completely dissolved. Add the evaporated milk and water and mix well.

Pour into a lightly buttered baking dish. Place the dish in a pan of water and bake in a 350° F. oven for 45 minutes. Serves 6.

MOLDED LEMON CREAM

2 eggs, separated
¾ cup granulated sugar
2 tablespoons lemon juice
2 teaspoons lemon rind, finely grated
1 tablespoon unflavored gelatin
¼ cup cold water
1 cup heavy whipping cream

Beat the egg yolks until they are light and lemon colored. Gradually add the sugar to the yolks and continue to beat until fluffy. Set aside.

Mix the lemon juice, lemon rind, gelatin and water together in a heat-proof mixing cup. Place the mixing cup in hot water over low heat and stir until the gelatin is dissolved.

Place the egg yolk mixture in the top of a double boiler along with the gelatin mixture and mix well. Cook over barely boiling water until the mixture thickens. Remove from the heat and cool to room temperature.

Beat the egg whites until they stand in peaks. Beat the whipping cream until it stands in peaks. Alternately fold the egg whites and the whipping cream into the cooled egg yolk mixture. Pour into a mold which has been rinsed with cold water and chill in the refrigerator for at least 4 hours. Unmold and serve. Serves 6.

SPIRITED CUSTARD

4 eggs, separated
1 ounce brandy
1 ounce rum
¾ cup granulated sugar
¼ cup cold water
1 tablespoon unflavored gelatin
1 cup whipping cream
1 teaspoon vanilla

Beat the egg yolks until they are lemon colored; add the brandy and rum. Continue to beat and sprinkle in the granulated sugar a little at a time. Beat until the mixture is creamy.

Place the cold water and the unflavored gelatin in a heat-proof cup for 5 minutes or until the gelatin is softened; then place the cup in a pan of slowly boiling water until the gelatin is completely dissolved. When dissolved, add the gelatin and water mixture to the egg yolk mixture. Beat until well mixed.

Beat the egg whites until they stand in peaks. Beat the whipping cream until it stands in peaks. Add the vanilla to the cream and beat for a second longer. Alternately fold in the whipped whites and the whipped cream into the egg yolk mixture. Pour into parfait glasses or sherbet glasses. Chill in the refrigerator for at least 3 hours before serving. Serves 6.

MEXICAN CUSTARD OR MEXICAN FLAN

1 tablespoon unflavored gelatin
3 cups whole milk
4 eggs, separated
½ cup granulated sugar
¼ teaspoon salt
¼ teaspoon vanilla
¼ teaspoon almond extract

Place the unflavored gelatin in 1 cup of the cold milk in a mixing bowl and allow it to soften.

Place the remaining two cups of milk in the top of a double boiler over rapidly boiling water. Cook until scalded. Mix the scalded milk with the gelatin and milk and stir until blended and the gelatin is completely dissolved.

Beat the egg yolks until lemon yellow; gradually add the sugar. Add ½ cup of the hot milk mixture and continue to beat for a few seconds. Add the egg yolk mixture to the milk and gelatin; mix well. Return the mixture to the top of the double boiler. Cook over slowly boiling water, stirring frequently, until the mixture coats the spoon. Stir in the salt, vanilla and almond extract. Remove from the heat and allow to cool to room temperature; then place in the refrigerator until thoroughly chilled; this should take about 1½ hours.

Beat the egg whites until they are stiff and stand in peaks. Gradually fold in the chilled custard mixture. Place in individual serving dishes or molds. Serve with whipped cream or with sugared fresh berries. Serves 6.

HEAVENLY DESSERT

4 eggs, separated and at room temperature
½ cup granulated sugar
1 ounce brandy
1 ounce rum
1 ounce creme de cacao
¼ cup cold water
1 tablespoon unflavored gelatin
1 cup whipping cream (thoroughly chilled)
1 teaspoon vanilla

Beat the egg yolks with a whisk or electric beater until they are light and lemon colored. Gradually add the sugar and continue beating until the mixture is creamy. Add the brandy, rum and creme de cacao and continue to beat after each addition. Set aside to allow the flavors to blend.

Place the gelatin in the cold water until softened; then place over slowly boiling water until the gelatin has completely dissolved. Stir the dissolved gelatin into the egg yolk mixture.

Beat the egg whites until they are stiff and stand in peaks. Fold the beaten whites into the yolk-gelatin mixture.

Whip the cream until it is stiff and stands in peaks; add the vanilla and fold the whipped cream into the egg yolk and white mixture. Spoon into tall glasses and chill in the refrigerator at least three hours before serving. Serves 6.

CHOCOLATE MOUSSE

2 2-ounce squares semi-sweet baking chocolate
¾ cup light brown sugar, lightly packed
2 tablespoons warm tap water
1 ounce good brandy
5 eggs, separated

Melt the chocolate in the top of a double boiler over slowly boiling water. Add the brown sugar and water and continue to cook, stirring constantly, until the sugar is dissolved.

Beat the egg yolks until they are mixed and slightly bubbly. Gradually add the egg yolks to the cooking chocolate mixture, beating constantly. Cook for 1 minute longer, beating constantly, and then remove from the heat. Allow to cool slightly and stir in the brandy. Set aside to cool.

Beat the egg whites until they stand in stiff peaks. Gently fold the beaten egg whites into the chocolate mixture taking care not to lose any of the air. Pour into individual parfait glasses and chill overnight in the refrigerator. Serves 6.

SNOW EGG PUDDING

6 eggs, separated
1¾ cups milk
¼ cup granulated sugar
1 teaspoon lemon juice
½ teaspoon vanilla
¼ cup brown sugar

Place the milk, granulated sugar, lemon juice and vanilla in a broad shallow saucepan or skillet over low heat. Stir so that all of the sugar is dissolved and does not stick to the bottom of the pan. Heat the milk mixture until it reaches a very slow boil.

Beat the egg whites until they begin to stand in peaks; add the brown sugar gradually and continue beating until they stand in firm peaks. Using a tablespoon, scoop up a portion of the egg mixture; level it off with a knife and then slip this "half egg" shaped egg white into the slowly boiling milk. Turn each "half egg" over once so that both sides are done evenly. Remove the "half eggs" to paper toweling and allow them to drain.

Strain the milk mixture into another bowl and allow to cool slightly. Beat the egg yolks until they are light and lemon colored. Slowly add the cooled milk mixture to the yolks and continue to beat for a second or two longer. Place the milk and egg yolk mixture in a saucepan over low heat and cook, stirring constantly, until the mixture has thickened and coats the spoon. Remove from the heat and allow to cool to room temperature. Pour into a suitable serving dish, and arrange the "half eggs" over the surface. Place in the refrigerator to chill for 1 hour. Serves 6.

EGG AND RICE CUSTARD

½ cup milk
¼ cup quick-cooking rice
1 tablespoon butter
4 eggs, separated
½ cup sugar
⅛ teaspoon almond extract
¼ cup almonds, finely chopped

Heat the milk in the top of a double boiler to just below the scalding point. Add the quick-cooking rice as it comes from the package. Stir and cover. Cook for 5 minutes longer or until the rice is puffed up and the mixture is quite thick. Remove from the heat, stir in the butter and set aside to cool to room temperature.

Beat the egg yolks until they are light and lemon colored. Add the sugar and beat again until the sugar is thoroughly mixed. Add to the rice mixture. Add the almond extract to the ground almonds and add to the rice mixture. Mix all thoroughly.

Beat the egg whites until they stand in firm peaks. Gently fold the egg whites into the rice mixture, taking care not to lose any of the air. Pour into a buttered baking dish and place in a 325° F. oven for 35 minutes or until the top is a delicate golden brown. Serve hot. If you wish, serve with chilled cream poured over the pudding or with a dab of whipped cream. Serves 4.

LEMON-CAKE-PUDDING

¼ cup soft butter
1 cup granulated sugar
4 eggs, separated
3 tablespoons all-purpose flour
¼ cup fresh lemon juice
2 teaspoons lemon peel, finely grated
¼ teaspoon salt
1 cup half-and-half cream
½ cup slivered almonds, lightly toasted

Cream the butter until it is light and fluffy; add the sugar gradually and continue to cream for a few seconds. Add the egg yolks, one at a time; beat after each addition. Add the flour, lemon juice, lemon peel and salt; beat again until all is thoroughly mixed. Add the half-and-half cream and ¼ cup of the almonds; mix and beat again. Set aside.

Beat the egg whites until they are stiff and stand in peaks. Fold into the mixture, taking great care to retain the air in the whites. Pour into a buttered loaf pan. Set the pan in another pan of hot water and bake at 325° F. for 35 minutes.

Then, increase the heat to 350° F. and bake for 8 minutes longer or until the top is a golden brown. Sprinkle the remaining ¼ cup almonds over the top while the dish is still hot.

Serve either warm or cool to room temperature and then chill in the refrigerator and serve. Serves 6 generously.

BAKED LEMON AND EGG CUSTARD

3 eggs, separated
1 cup granulated sugar
1 tablespoon all-purpose flour
1 cup milk
1 2-inch diameter lemon

Place the egg yolks in a 1½-quart mixing bowl and beat until they are lemon colored. Mix the sugar and flour together thoroughly; add a tablespoonful at a time to the egg yolks and continue beating after each addition.

Add the milk a little at a time and beat after each addition. Grate the outside rind of the lemon until you have a teaspoon of it; then squeeze the lemon. Add the grated rind and the juice gradually to the mixture; continue to beat after each addition.

Beat the egg whites until they stand in peaks. Carefully fold the beaten egg whites into the yolk mixture. Pour into a 1½-quart buttered baking dish. Place in a pan of water in a 325° F. oven for 25 minutes. Place a sheet of aluminum foil, glossy side down, on the oven shelf immediately above the pudding. This foil will reflect the steam and keep the top of the pudding soft. Do not cover the actual baking dish with the foil, as this prevents the pudding from rising to its fullest and holds in too much steam.

Remove from the oven and serve hot. Top with whipped, sweetened cream if you desire. Serves 4.

BUTTERSCOTCH EGG PUDDING

2 cups milk
3 cups soft bread crumbs made from enriched white bread
¼ cup butter
½ cup dark brown sugar
3 eggs
¼ teaspoon salt
1 teaspoon cinnamon
½ cup seedless raisins

Place the milk in the top of a double boiler and scald over rapidly boiling water. Remove from the heat and add the bread crumbs. Mix well. Add the butter and sugar and mix again. Set aside to cool to room temperature.

Beat the eggs until mixed and bubbly; add the beaten eggs, salt, cinnamon and raisins to the bread crumb and milk mixture and beat slightly.

Place in a well buttered baking dish. Place the dish in a pan of hot water and bake at 350° F. for 45 minutes. Serve at once with sweetened whipped cream or a topping of hard sauce. (See Chapter XIII for hard sauce recipe.) Serves 6.

SO GOOD PUDDING

1 cup granulated sugar
½ cup butter
3 eggs
¾ cup milk
1 tablespoon all-purpose flour
½ teaspoon baking powder
1 cup dates, snipped into small pieces
½ cup pecans, coarsely chopped
1 cup chilled whipping cream
1 tablespoon powdered sugar
½ teaspoon rum flavoring or 1 teaspoon vanilla

Cream the sugar and butter together until light and fluffy. Beat the eggs until they are light and lemon colored; add the beaten eggs to the butter and sugar and beat for a few seconds. Gradually add the milk; sprinkle in the flour and baking powder. Mix well. Stir in the dates and pecans.

Pour the mixture into a 9-inch square buttered baking dish.

Bake in a 350° F. oven for 45 minutes. Remove from the oven and allow to cool slightly. Cut into 6 portions.

Beat the cream until it just begins to stand in peaks; add the sugar and rum flavoring and continue beating until the cream stands in peaks. Serve a portion of the rum-flavored cream over each portion of the pudding. Serves 6.

LITTLE LEMON PUDDINGS

½ cup granulated sugar
2 tablespoons all-purpose flour
½ teaspoon salt
3 eggs, separated
1 cup milk
2 tablespoons lemon juice
2 teaspoons lemon rind, finely grated

Mix the sugar, flour and salt together. Set aside.

Beat the egg yolks until they are light and lemon colored. Continue beating and gradually add the milk, lemon juice and lemon rind; then add the sugar-flour mixture a little at a time. Continue to beat until smooth and creamy.

Beat the egg whites until they are stiff and stand in peaks. Fold the whites into the yolk mixture, taking great care to retain all the air.

Pour the mixture into six lightly buttered custard cups. Place the custard cups in a pan of hot water and bake at 350° F. for ½ hour. Remove from the oven and chill in the refrigerator for at least 1 hour before serving. Serves 6.

VANILLA CUSTARD

1 cup milk
1 cup half-and-half cream
3 egg yolks (see Chapter XIII for using left-over whites)
1 cup light brown sugar, lightly packed
1 teaspoon vanilla

Bring the milk and half-and-half cream to a boil for 1 second and then remove from the heat and allow to cool to room temperature.

Beat the egg yolks until they are light and lemon colored. Gradually add the brown sugar, beating after each addition. Continue to beat and gradually add the cooled milk.

Place the mixture in a double boiler over slowly boiling water. Cook, stirring constantly, until the mixture thickens and coats the spoon. Add the vanilla.

Pour into a lightly buttered mold or into individual serving glasses; place in the refrigerator and chill for 2 hours. Serves 6.

This custard may be served with a dab of whipped cream and a maraschino cherry to give it added glamour. It is also a good companion to sugared chopped strawberries or raspberries.

Chapter IX

THE EGG AND PIE

PIES MADE WITH eggs are a delight to serve. When the price of fresh or canned fruits for pie soars way out of your family's budget, try making some of the egg-rich pies in this chapter. They will be a welcome change, and you will get many requests for repeat performances.

Egg-rich pies serve another purpose too; they give you a chance to slip extra protein and vitamins into the daily fare.

MERINGUE PEACH PIE

4 egg whites (see Chapter XIV for using left-over yolks)
⅔ cup granulated sugar
½ cup powdered sugar
½ teaspoon vanilla
1 #2 can peach slices, drained thoroughly and chilled
1 cup chilled whipping cream
1 tablespoon (additional) powdered sugar
½ teaspoon (additional) vanilla

Beat the egg whites until they begin to stand in peaks. Gradually add both the granulated sugar and the powdered sugar. Beat after each addition. Add the vanilla and mix well. Liberally butter a 9-inch pie tin and spread the meringue over the bottom and sides. Build the meringue up slightly around the edges. Place in a 300° F. oven and bake for 1 hour or until set and crisp. Remove from the oven and let cool to room temperature.

Using a very sharp knife, score the surface of the meringue into 6 suitable wedges, bringing the cutting marks out to the edge. Do not go through to the bottom. Place the drained peach slices in the center of the meringue.

Whip the cream until it begins to stand in peaks; add the additional powdered sugar and vanilla and whip a few seconds longer. Spread the whipped cream over the top of the pie. Chill for about 15 minutes in the refrigerator. Cut into wedges, following your previous markings. Serves 6.

EGG-RICH PIE CRUST

Since most pies start with the crust, this egg-rich pie crust is heading the top of our list. If your family is tired of the old-fashioned shortening, flour and salt type of crust, try this on your next pie.

2½ cups all-purpose flour
1½ teaspoons granulated sugar
¼ teaspoon salt
1 cup vegetable shortening
2 egg yolks (see Chapter XIII for using left-over whites)
Ice water

Mix the flour, sugar and salt together thoroughly in a mixing bowl. Add the shortening; using a pastry blender or two table knives, cut the shortening into the flour until the mixture is the consistency of coarse corn meal.

Place the egg yolks in a measuring cup without breaking them. Add enough ice water to make 1 cup. Stir the yolks and water together until they are thoroughly mixed and then add to the flour mixture. Mix together gently until it forms a ball.

Place the ball of dough on a lightly floured pastry cloth or board and roll out to the desired size. Bake for 12 minutes in a pre-heated 475° F. oven or until the bottom and sides of the crust are a rich golden brown.

This recipe makes the top and bottom for a 9-inch pie. Halve the recipe if you require only the bottom crust. Since this is a rich pie crust, it may separate when transferred to a baking pan. If it does, press together against the sides of the pan.

SQUARE PINEAPPLE PIE
OR UNBAKED PINEAPPLE PIE

2 tablespoons soft butter
½ pound vanilla wafers, crushed to the consistency of rice
1½ cups powdered sugar
½ cup (additional) butter, at room temperature
3 eggs
1 cup whipping cream, whipped and chilled
1 13½-ounce can crushed pineapple, drained very dry

With the 2 tablespoons of soft butter, lavishly butter a 10-inch square pan. Sprinkle all but ½ cup of the vanilla wafer crumbs over the bottom of the pan. Set aside.

Cream the powdered sugar and the ½ cup butter together until light and fluffy. Add the eggs one at a time, beating after each addition. Continue to beat until the mixture is light and airy. Spread this mixture over the vanilla wafer crumbs in the bottom of the pan.

Fold the whipped cream and the drained pineapple together and spread over the sugar and butter mixture in the pan. Sprinkle the top with the ½ cup of reserved vanilla wafer crumbs. Chill in the refrigerator at least three hours. Serves 8.

HEAVENLY LEMON PIE

1 9-inch baked pie shell
6 eggs
1 cup granulated sugar
⅓ cup lemon juice
2 teaspoons lemon rind, finely grated
½ cup (additional) granulated sugar

Separate the eggs; place 3 of the whites in one bowl for beating and adding to the pie filling. Reserve the 3 remaining whites for the meringue.

Beat the six egg yolks until they are mixed and bubbly. Gradually add the sugar and continue beating; add the lemon juice and grated rind and beat for 1 minute longer.

Place the egg yolk mixture in the top of a double boiler and cook, stirring constantly, over barely boiling water until it thickens and coats a spoon. Remove from the heat and cool while you beat the three whites until they stand in peaks. Fold the beaten egg whites into the slightly cooled egg yolk mixture. Pour the mixture into the pastry shell. Allow to cool 5 minutes longer.

Beat the three remaining egg whites until they just begin to get glossy; gradually add the ½ cup sugar, and continue to beat until it stands in shiny peaks. Using a rubber spoon, spread the meringue over the top of the pie. Place in a 325° F. oven for 12 minutes or until the tips of the meringue just begin to turn a golden brown. Allow the pie to cool to room temperature before cutting. Serves 6.

LEMON PIE SANS MERINGUE

1 9-inch baked pie shell
3 eggs, separated
½ cup granulated sugar
1 teaspoon all-purpose flour
¼ cup fresh lemon juice
2 teaspoons lemon rind, finely grated
¼ cup boiling water
½ cup (additional) granulated sugar

Place the egg yolks in a bowl and beat until light and lemon colored. Add the sugar, flour, lemon juice and lemon rind and beat again until all is thoroughly mixed. Place the mixture in the top of a double boiler; stir in the ¼ cup boiling water and mix well. Cook the mixture over slowly boiling water, stirring constantly, until it has thickened and coats a spoon. Remove from the heat and cool quickly by replacing the boiling water in the bottom of the boiler with ice water. Stir occasionally while the mixture is cooling.

Beat the egg whites until they stand in peaks. Gradually add the additional ½ cup sugar and continue to beat for a few seconds longer. Fold the egg white mixture into the lemon custard. Pour into the baked pie shell and place in a 350° F. oven for 8 minutes or until the top has turned a delicate golden brown. Remove from the oven and allow to cool to room temperature before cutting. Cut into wedges. Serves 6.

PECAN PIE

1 9-inch unbaked pie shell
½ cup butter
1 cup granulated sugar
4 eggs
¾ cup dark corn syrup
½ teaspoon salt
1 teaspoon vanilla
1½ cups pecans, coarsely chopped; reserve about 12 pecan
  halves for decorating the top of the pie

Cream the butter until soft; add the sugar gradually and continue to cream until the mixture is light and fluffy.

Beat the eggs with a whisk or rotary beater until they are blended and slightly bubbly. Add the beaten eggs alternately with the dark corn syrup to the sugar and butter mixture.

Beat slightly after each addition. Add the salt and the vanilla. Stir in the chopped pecans.

Pour into the unbaked pie shell and place in a 375° F. oven for 30 minutes. Sprinkle the pecan halves over the top and return to the oven for an additional 15 minutes or until the pie is firm in the center and a rich brown color. Remove from the oven and cool to room temperature before serving. Place in the refrigerator for 1 hour if you desire picture-perfect wedges. Serves 6.

PINEAPPLE CUSTARD PIE

1 9-inch baked pie shell
2 cups crushed pineapple, drained
1 cup granulated sugar
2 eggs, separated
1 tablespoon butter
¼ cup (additional) sugar

Place the pineapple and sugar in the top of a double boiler and mix thoroughly. Beat the egg yolks until they are thoroughly mixed. Add them to the pineapple mixture and mix thoroughly. Place the top of the double boiler over rapidly boiling water and cook, stirring constantly, until the mixture has thickened. Remove from heat and add the butter. Mix, and then allow to cool for 5 minutes.

Pour the pineapple mixture into the baked pie crust and spread evenly with a rubber spoon.

Beat the egg whites until they stand in peaks. Gradually add the additional ¼ cup sugar and beat again until all is mixed. Spread the meringue over the top of the pineapple filling making sure you bring it out to the edges, completely sealing and covering the pineapple custard. Place in a 325° F. oven for 15 to 20 minutes or until the meringue has turned a golden brown. Allow to cool before cutting. Serves 6.

OLD-FASHIONED PLAIN CUSTARD PIE

1 unbaked 9-inch pie shell
3 eggs
4 tablespoons granulated sugar
⅛ teaspoon salt
3 cups scalding hot milk
¼ teaspoon freshly grated nutmeg

Beat the eggs until they are thoroughly mixed and bubbly. Add the sugar and salt and mix well. Add three tablespoons of the scalding hot milk to the egg mixture; mix well and then add the egg mixture to the milk. Beat again until all is evenly mixed.

Pour the mixture into the unbaked 9-inch pie shell and place in a 450° F. oven for 10 minutes. Then, reduce the heat to 350° F. and bake for 20 minutes or until a knife inserted in the middle comes out clean. Remove from the oven and sprinkle with nutmeg. Allow the pie to cool to room temperature before cutting. Serves 6.

PRUNE AND CUSTARD PIE

1 9-inch unbaked pie shell
2 eggs
1 cup scalded milk
1 tablespoon all-purpose flour
½ cup granulated sugar
1 tablespoon butter
¼ teaspoon cinnamon
¼ teaspoon freshly grated nutmeg
1 cup cooked prunes, drained, halved and pitted

Beat the eggs until they are light and lemon colored; gradually add the scalded milk, beating after each addition. Sprinkle in the flour and sugar and continue to beat until mixed and free of any lumps. Add the butter, cinnamon and nutmeg and beat again until all is mixed.

Stir in the prune halves and then pour the mixture into the unbaked pie shell. Bake in a 450° F. oven for 10 minutes and then reduce the heat to 350° F. Bake for an additional 20 minutes or until a knife comes out clean when inserted in the center of the pie. Allow to cool to room temperature before serving. Serves 6.

COCONUT CREAM PIE

1 9-inch baked pie shell
5 eggs, separated
1¼ cups granulated sugar
¼ teaspoon salt
¼ cup cornstarch
2¾ cups milk
2 teaspoons vanilla
¼ cup butter
1 10-ounce can grated moist coconut
¼ cup (additional) granulated sugar

Beat the yolks until light and lemon colored. Set aside. Mix the sugar, salt and cornstarch together thoroughly. Scald the milk in the top of a double boiler. Add the sugar mixture to the milk and beat until free of lumps. Add three tablespoons of the hot milk mixture to the egg yolks, mix and then add the yolks to the hot milk. Beat again until thoroughly mixed. Cook over boiling water, stirring constantly, until the mixture has thickened and coats the spoon. Remove from the heat and allow to cool slightly.

Mix the vanilla and the butter together. Add ¾ of the can of coconut and mix very well. (Reserve the remaining coconut for the meringue topping.) Stir the coconut mixture into the milk mixture. When blended, pour into the baked pie shell.

Beat the egg whites until they begin to stand in peaks. Gradually add the additional ¼ cup sugar and continue beating until the mixture stands in firm peaks. Cover the pie with the meringue, making sure you bring it out to the edges, completely sealing and covering the custard. Sprinkle the remaining ¼ can of coconut over the top of the meringue. Bake in a 325° F. oven for 20 minutes or until the top has turned a golden brown. Cool before cutting. Serves 6.

LEMON PIE

1 9-inch baked pie shell
2 cups milk
1 cup granulated sugar
¼ teaspoon salt
¼ cup cornstarch
3 eggs, separated
1 tablespoon grated lemon rind
¼ cup lemon juice
¼ cup (additional) granulated sugar

Scald the milk in the top of a double boiler; allow to cool slightly. Mix the sugar, salt and cornstarch together thoroughly. Add to the scalded milk; beat with a whisk or rotary beater until free of lumps. Cook over rapidly boiling water, stirring constantly, for 10 minutes or until the mixture has thickened and begins to coat a spoon.

Beat the egg yolks until they are light and lemon colored. Take several spoonfuls of the milk mixture and add it to the egg yolks; then mix the yolks into the thickened mixture. Beat for a second or so to mix well. Cook, stirring constantly, for 5 additional minutes. Remove from the heat and add the lemon rind and lemon juice, mix well. Allow to cool for 5 minutes and then pour into the baked pie shell.

Beat the egg whites until they stand in peaks. Gradually add the additional ¼ cup sugar and beat again. Using a rubber spoon, spread the meringue over the lemon pie filling. Bring to the edges of the crust, sealing the filling all the way around.

Place in a 325° F. oven for 15 to 20 minutes or until the peaks of the meringue begin to turn a golden brown. Cool to room temperature before cutting. Serves 6.

Chapter X

EGG CAKES AND PANCAKES

GRANTED, ONE OF today's most convenient foods is the packaged cake and pancake mix. These mixes are good and, for the most part, absolutely foolproof. In most cases, all one needs is tap water, a measuring cup, a bowl and pans for baking. However, if you have not made your own egg-rich cakes and pancakes, you are missing a lot of fun.

Most commercial cake and egg pancake mixes depend upon powdered eggs for their leavening agent, along with other ingredients. By comparison, this is like trying to make canned peas taste like fresh ones.

This chapter contains cakes and pancakes which, for the most part, contain four or more eggs. Eggs are the protein perfect food; you can slip extra protein into your family's diet in the form of a delicious cake or a hearty breakfast of egg-rich pancakes. Putting forth this little extra effort of starting from scratch will bring you accolades of praise and pleas for more of the same.

DUTCH EGG PANCAKES

6 eggs
2 cups half-and-half cream
½ teaspoon salt
½ cup all-purpose flour
1 cup light brown sugar

Beat the eggs with a rotary or electric beater until they are very frothy and bubbly. Add the half-and-half cream and the salt and beat for a few seconds longer.

While slowly beating, add the flour gradually.

Bake on a buttered griddle in very thin pancakes. As each cake is done, sprinkle a portion of the brown sugar over the surface and then roll up jelly-roll fashion. Place in a buttered baking dish in a 300° F. oven until all the pancakes are done. Serve with additional brown sugar and butter or syrup. Makes 1 dozen 6-inch pancakes. Serves 6, allowing 2 pancakes per person.

EGG CUSTARD CAKE

10 eggs
⅛ teaspoon salt
1 teaspoon cream of tartar
1½ cups granulated sugar
1 cup cake flour

Filling and Frosting:
¾ cup granulated sugar
1½ cups half-and-half cream
1 tablespoon unflavored gelatin
¼ cup cold water
2 cups chilled whipping cream
1 teaspoon vanilla

Separate the eggs 5 at a time. Place 5 of the yolks in one bowl and set aside. Place the 10 whites in another bowl and the 5 remaining yolks in still another bowl.

Add the salt to the 10 egg whites and beat until they begin to get glossy and stand in peaks. Add the cream of tartar and continue to beat until they stand in firm peaks.

Beat 5 of the egg yolks until they are light and lemon colored. Add the sugar and beat again. Into these 5 beaten egg yolks and sugar, fold in half of the beaten egg whites alternately with small portions of the flour. When you have added all of the flour, fold in the remainder of the beaten egg whites. Pour into a lightly buttered 10-inch tube pan and place in a 200° F. oven.

Bake for 15 minutes at 200° F.; increase the heat to 225° F. and bake 15 minutes longer; increase the heat to 250° F., and bake 15 minutes longer; then increase the heat to 300° F. and bake for 30 minutes more, for a total baking time of 1 hour and 15 minutes. Remove from the oven, invert the pan and allow to cool.

For the filling and the topping, beat the 5 remaining egg yolks until very light and frothy; add the sugar and beat again. Place the half-and-half cream in the top of a double boiler and heat to just below the scalding point.

Soften the gelatin in the cold water and set aside.

Add the beaten yolks and sugar to the hot half-and-half cream a little at a time. Cook over low heat, stirring constantly, until the mixture is thick and coats the spoon. Add the softened gelatin and stir until all of the gelatin is dissolved. Remove the top of the double boiler from the hot water and allow the custard to cool to room temperature.

Beat the whipping cream until it stands in peaks. Add the vanilla and beat for one second longer. Fold the stiffly beaten cream into the custard.

Remove the cake from the tube pan and cut horizontally into two layers. Spread the top of the bottom layer with a portion of the custard. Cover with the other layer and proceed to frost the entire cake with the custard. Chill in the refrigerator for 1 hour before serving. Serves 8 generously. Store any left-overs of this cake under refrigeration.

CHOCOLATE CHEESE CAKE

1½ cups graham cracker crumbs, finely crushed
½ cup melted butter
1 6-ounce package chocolate chips
1 8-ounce package cream cheese, at room temperature
½ cup granulated sugar
1 teaspoon vanilla
½ teaspoon salt
3 eggs, separated
¼ cup (additional) granulated sugar
½ pint chilled whipping cream

Mix the graham cracker crumbs and the melted butter together thoroughly and then line the bottom and sides of a 9-inch pie tin. Press the crumbs down firmly and place in the refrigerator to chill.

Melt the chocolate chips in a double boiler over rapidly boiling water. Add the cream cheese to the chocolate chips along with the sugar, vanilla and salt. Using a whisk or rotary beater, beat the mixture until it is fluffy and blended. Beat the egg yolks until they are light and lemon colored; add a tablespoon of the hot cheese mixture to the eggs and then add the eggs to the cheese mixture. Beat again until smoothly blended. Remove from the heat and allow to cool to room temperature.

Beat the egg whites until they stand in stiff peaks. Add the additional sugar and mix well. Fold the sweetened egg whites into the cheese mixture. Beat the cream until it stands in peaks and then fold into the cheese mixture. Place in the chilled graham cracker crust and freeze until firm. Remove from the freezer 10 minutes before serving. Serves 8.

23-MINUTE ANGEL CAKE

Here is a recipe for the simplest angel cake I have ever had the pleasure of making. It is practically foolproof, fall-proof and very delicious.

1½ cups egg whites at room temperature (approximately 1 dozen eggs, depending upon their size)
1 teaspoon cream of tartar
¼ teaspoon salt
1 cup sifted granulated sugar
1 teaspoon vanilla
½ teaspoon almond extract
1 cup cake flour
1 cup powdered sugar

Preheat the oven to 425° F. Place an ungreased angel food pan in the oven while it is preheating. The preheating of the pan is vitally important to the success and high-rise nature of this cake.

Beat the egg whites with a rotary beater, whisk or electric beater at slow speed. When the whites just begin to turn glossy and bubbly, add the cream of tartar and salt. Continue to beat for a second or two to mix well. Continue beating and sprinkle in a tablespoon of the sifted granulated sugar at a time. As you beat and add the sugar, the whites will begin to stand in peaks. Before adding the last two tablespoons of sugar, add the vanilla and the almond extract. Then continue to beat until the whites stand in glossy peaks.

Sift the cake flour and the powdered sugar together six times and start adding this mixture, two tablespoons at a time, to the egg white mixture, beating constantly.

When all of the powdered sugar and flour have been incorporated into the egg white mixture, spoon the mixture into the hot, preheated angel food pan with a rubber spoon. Use the rubber spoon to gently smooth out the top of the cake.

Place the pan back in the 425° F. oven and bake for exactly 23 minutes. Do not open the oven door during this period.

At the end of the baking period, remove the cake from the oven and invert immediately. If you do not have an angel food pan with legs for suspension, invert the cake over a large soda bottle by sticking the neck of the bottle in the center tube.

Allow the cake to cool to room temperature. Loosen the outer edge with a sharp pointed knife and turn out on a suitable cake plate.

This cake may be frosted with a simple white 7-minute frosting, a glaze or may be topped with strawberries and whipped cream. This cake is also delicious with a simple dusting of powdered sugar. Serves 8 to 10.

BASIC ANGEL CAKE

1½ cups granulated sugar
1 cup sifted cake flour
½ teaspoon salt
1½ teaspoons cream of tartar
1½ cups egg whites (approximately 1 dozen eggs)
1 teaspoon vanilla

Sift the granulated sugar three times, and then divide the sugar in half. Place half of the sugar with the cake flour and sift together 5 times.

Mix the salt and the cream of tartar together well and set aside. Start beating the egg whites until they are bubbly and then sprinkle the salt and cream of tartar mixture over the top. Again beat until the egg whites are shiny and just starting to stand up in peaks. Add the vanilla and 2 tablespoons of the granulated sugar. Continue to beat. Add more of the sugar and beat; continue until all the sugar is used up.

After you have added all of the sugar, start folding in the sugar-flour mixture ¼ cup at a time. Continue to add and fold until all is smooth and well mixed.

Using a rubber spoon, place the mixture in a 10-inch ungreased angel food pan. Smooth the surface with the rubber spoon, taking care not to force the air out of the batter. Place in a 350° F. oven for 40 minutes. The top of the cake should be a golden brown and spring back to the touch when it is done.

Invert the cake on a rack for 1 hour. Remove by inserting a sharp knife around the edge of the pan when the cake is cooled. Frost with your favorite frosting or whipped cream and berries. Serves 8 to 10.

FILLED EGG PANCAKES WITH SAUCE

Filling:
2 cups creamed cottage cheese
½ teaspoon grated lemon rind
¼ cup sugar

Pancakes:
4 eggs
1 cup half-and-half cream
1 cup all-purpose flour
1 teaspoon salt
1 tablespoon granulated sugar
¼ cup butter, vegetable oil or shortening for frying

Topping:
1 #300 can dark, pitted cherries in heavy syrup
2 tablespoons water
2 tablespoons cornstarch
1 teaspoon fresh lemon juice

Mix the cottage cheese, lemon rind and sugar together thoroughly. Set aside for the flavors to unite.

Beat the eggs slightly with a rotary beater. Add ½ cup of the cream. Add ½ cup of the flour, the salt and the granulated sugar. Continue to beat until all is smooth. Add the remainder of the flour and the cream and beat again until all is smooth.

Melt 1 teaspoon of the butter or shortening in a skillet over moderate heat. Pour ¼ cup of the batter into the middle of the skillet and then tip the skillet in all directions so that the batter runs towards the outside, forming a thin pancake. Fry on both sides until a golden brown. Remove to a board; place a scant ¼ cup of the flavored cottage cheese mixture on one edge of the pancake and roll up jelly-roll fashion. Place on a heated platter, cover with foil and keep warm in a 200° F. oven until you have fried and filled all of the pancakes in this manner.

Drain the cherries through a sieve and place the juice in a saucepan over moderate heat. Mix the cornstarch and the water together until you have a smooth paste. Stir this into the cherry juice and cook until thickened and transparent. Add the cherries and lemon juice and continue to cook about 5 minutes longer, until the cherries are warmed through.

Pour the heated cherries and part of their thickened sauce over the filled pancake rolls. Serve at once, piping hot. Serve the remainder of the sauce as a pass-around syrup. Serves 6, allowing 2 pancakes per person.

CHOCOLATE ICEBOX CAKE

4 squares bitter chocolate
¾ cup granulated sugar
⅓ cup half-and-half cream
6 eggs, separated
1½ cups butter
1½ cups confectioners sugar
1 teaspoon vanilla
3 dozen lady fingers, halved lengthwise
1 cup whipping cream, chilled and whipped
½ bar German sweet chocolate, grated

Melt the bitter chocolate in the top of a double boiler over rapidly boiling water. When melted, remove from the heat. Mix the sugar, cream and egg yolks together; beat until smooth and then gradually stir into the melted chocolate in the top of the double boiler. Return the double boiler to the heat and cook the mixture, stirring constantly, until thickened. Set aside to cool.

Cream the butter until smooth; gradually add 1 cup of the sugar and continue to cream until light and fluffy. Reserve the remainder of the sugar until later. Add the cooled chocolate mixture to the butter and the sugar mixture. Beat until light and fluffy. Add the vanilla.

Beat the egg whites until they stand in peaks; beat in the remaining ½ cup confectioners sugar. Fold the sweetened egg whites into the chocolate mixture.

Line the bottom and sides of a lightly buttered spring form pan with the lady finger halves (crisp side out). Pour ⅓ of the chocolate mixture into the lined spring form. Follow this with a few of the lady finger halves. Repeat until all is used up. Chill in the refrigerator at least 6 hours or overnight.

To unmold, remove the outer ring of the spring form pan. Loosen the cake from the bottom with a broad spatula and then carefully slide the chilled cake on to a cake plate and garnish the top and sides with the whipped cream. Sprinkle the sweet grated chocolate over the whipped cream. Serves 8 generously.

EGG-RICH CHEESE CAKE #1

Crust:
10 graham crackers
¼ cup melted butter
¼ cup granulated sugar
⅛ teaspoon cinnamon

Filling:
2 8-ounce packages cream cheese, at room temperature
4 eggs, separated
½ cup granulated sugar
½ teaspoon vanilla

Topping:
2 cups sour cream
¼ cup granulated sugar
½ teaspoon vanilla

Crush the graham crackers until they are very fine. Add the melted butter, sugar and cinnamon. Mix thoroughly. Press the mixture over the bottom and sides of a 9-inch pie pan. Chill in the refrigerator for at least 1 hour.

Place the cream cheese and the egg yolks together in a mixing bowl and beat until thoroughly mixed and light. Add the sugar and vanilla and beat again for a few seconds. Beat the egg whites until they are glossy and stand in peaks. Fold the egg whites into the cheese and egg yolk mixture. Pour into the chilled graham cracker crust. Bake in a 350° F. oven for 25 minutes. Remove from the oven and allow to cool for ½ hour.

Mix the sour cream, sugar and vanilla thoroughly. Carefully spread this mixture over the top of the cooled cheese cake. Bake again in a 450° F. oven for 5 minutes. Remove from the oven and cool to room temperature; chill in the refrigerator at least 4 hours before serving. Serves 8.

EGG-RICH CHEESE CAKE #2

Crust:
1 cup graham cracker crumbs, finely crushed
½ cup melted butter
¼ cup granulated sugar

Filling:
6 eggs, separated
1 cup granulated sugar
2 tablespoons cornstarch
3 8-ounce packages cream cheese, at room temperature
1 cup sour cream
1 cup half-and-half cream
1 teaspoon cream of tartar
1 teaspoon vanilla

Mix the crushed graham cracker crumbs, butter and sugar thoroughly. Line the bottom and sides of a lavishly buttered spring form pan with the crumb mixture. Chill in the refrigerator while you are making the filling.

Preheat the oven to 350° F. Beat the egg yolks until they are frothy and lemon colored. Gradually add the sugar and the cornstarch. Beat after each addition. Add the cream cheese, sour cream and half-and-half cream. Continue to beat for 5 minutes, scraping the sides of the bowl from time to time to assure thorough mixing. Then add the cream of tartar and vanilla to the yolk mixture. Mix well.

Beat the egg whites until they are stiff and stand in peaks. Fold the egg whites into the yolk mixture, taking great care to retain all the air. Pour into the chilled, graham cracker-lined spring form. Place in the pre-heated 350° F. oven for 1 hour. Then, turn the oven off, do not open and let the cake stand in the hot oven for an additional hour. Remove and let cool to room temperature before cutting. Serves 8.

EGG-RICH CHEESE CAKE #3

Crust:
2 cups fine zwieback crumbs
¼ cup melted butter
¼ cup sugar
¼ teaspoon powdered cinnamon

Filling:
½ cup granulated sugar
2 tablespoons all-purpose flour
¼ teaspoon salt
2 8-ounce packages cream cheese, at room temperature
5 eggs, separated
1 teaspoon vanilla
1 cup heavy whipping cream
¼ teaspoon cream of tartar

Mix the zwieback crumbs, butter, sugar and cinnamon together well. Place over the bottom and sides of a lavishly buttered 10-inch spring form pan. Chill in the refrigerator for ¾ hour.

Mix the sugar, flour and salt together. Beat the softened cream cheese with a whisk, rotary beater or an electric beater at low speed. As it is beating, alternately add 1 egg yolk at a time and a small portion of the flour mixture. Continue to beat until all of the egg yolks and flour have been used up. Add the vanilla and gradually add the heavy cream. Continue to beat until all is thoroughly mixed and well blended. Set aside.

Beat the egg whites until they begin to get bubbly. Add the cream of tartar; continue to beat until the egg whites are shiny and stand in peaks but are not dry.

Using a rubber spoon, gently fold the egg whites into the yolk mixture. Pour the entire mixture into the chilled, crumb-lined pan.

Place in a 325° F. oven for 1 hour or until the center is firm to the touch. Remove from the oven and cool in the crumb-lined pan before attempting to remove the outer ring. Serves 8 to 10.

EGG YOLK PANCAKES

4 egg yolks (see Chapter XIII for using left-over whites)
1 tablespoon sugar
½ teaspoon salt
1 tablespoon melted butter
2 cups half-and-half cream
1¼ cups all-purpose flour
1 teaspoon baking powder

Beat the egg yolks until they are light and lemon colored. Gradually add the sugar, salt, melted butter and 1 cup of the half-and-half cream. Continue to beat until smooth.

Sift the flour and baking powder together twice; gradually add to the egg mixture, beating after each addition of flour. When you have added the rest of the flour, add the remaining cup of cream and mix well.

Bake on a lightly greased, hot griddle; serve with syrup or fresh fruit. Makes 12 large pancakes. Serves 6, allowing 2 pancakes per person.

OATMEAL PANCAKES

1½ cups "quick" rolled oats
2 cups buttermilk
½ cup all-purpose flour
1 teaspoon sugar
1 teaspoon baking soda
2 eggs, separated

Mix the rolled oats with the buttermilk and allow to stand for 15 minutes.

Gradually beat in the flour, sugar and baking soda. Beat the mixture well after each addition.

Beat the egg yolks until they are light and lemon colored and then add to the buttermilk and oat mixture. Mix well.

Beat the egg whites until they stand in peaks. Fold the whites into the mixture, taking care not to lose any of the air.

Bake the pancakes on a hot, lightly greased griddle. Makes 1 dozen large pancakes. Serves 6, allowing 2 pancakes per person. These are delicious served with butter and brown sugar or with maple syrup.

EGG PANCAKES WITH SOUR CREAM

3 eggs
½ cup sour cream
1 cup buttermilk
½ teaspoon baking soda
½ teaspoon salt
1 tablespoon granulated sugar
1½ cups all-purpose flour
2 teaspoons double action baking powder

Beat the eggs with a rotary or electric beater until they are well mixed and frothy. While still beating, add the sour cream and ½ cup of the buttermilk. Continue to beat until the mixture is bubbly.

Mix the soda, salt, sugar, flour and baking powder together and sift twice. Gradually add them to the egg and buttermilk mixture, beating after each addition. Then, add the remaining ½ cup of buttermilk.

Bake in large-sized pancakes on a hot, lightly greased griddle. Makes 1 dozen good-sized pancakes. Serves 6, allowing 2 pancakes per person.

RAW POTATO PANCAKES WITH EGGS

3 eggs, separated
2 3-inch diameter raw potatoes, scrubbed, but not peeled; grated
½ teaspoon salt
1 tablespoon granulated sugar
2 tablespoons all-purpose flour
½ teaspoon baking powder

Beat the egg yolks until light and lemon colored. Add the grated potatoes, salt, sugar, flour and baking powder. Mix all thoroughly.

Beat the egg whites until they stand in peaks; fold the beaten whites into the potato mixture taking care not to lose the air.

Fry on a lightly greased griddle in 3-inch diameter pancakes. Makes 1 dozen pancakes. Serve with applesauce and country sausages.

GERMAN EGG PANCAKE

4 eggs
⅓ cup milk
⅓ cup cake flour
½ teaspoon salt
2 tablespoons butter
1 3-inch diameter tart apple, peeled, cored and sliced paper thin

About 15 minutes before you start the pancake, preheat the oven to 375° F.

Beat the eggs for 1 minute, add the milk, flour and salt; continue to beat until the mixture is smooth.

Place the butter in an oven-proof iron skillet. Heat in the oven for 5 minutes or until the butter is melted and bubbly. Rotate the skillet from side to side so that the butter has coated the entire interior of the skillet.

Pour the egg batter into the hot buttered skillet; lightly sprinkle the apple slices over the top and place, uncovered, in the preheated oven for 25 minutes.

The edges of the pancake should be ruffled up and the center fairly firm; the top should be a light golden brown.

Serve in generous wedges with powdered sugar and wedges of lemon on the side. Serves 4.

3-EGG FEATHER CAKE

3 eggs, separated
⅛ teaspoon salt
½ cup boiling water
1½ cups granulated sugar
1½ cups cake flour
1 teaspoon lemon extract
1 teaspoon almond extract

Beat the egg yolks until they are light and lemon colored. Add the salt and mix thoroughly. Alternately add the boiling water, sugar and flour, a little at a time. Beat vigorously after each addition. Add the lemon and almond extract and beat again.

Beat the egg whites until they stand in peaks and carefully fold them into the batter. Pour into an ungreased angel food pan and bake in a 350° F. oven for 45 minutes or until the center is firm to the touch. Invert the pan and cool to room temperature. Frost with a sprinkling of powdered sugar. Serves 8.

ONE-EGG, ONE-BOWL CHOCOLATE CUPCAKES

1 square bitter baking chocolate
2 tablespoons butter
1 egg
¾ cup milk
1 cup sugar
1 teaspoon baking soda
1 teaspoon baking powder
1¼ cups all-purpose flour
½ teaspoon salt
1 teaspoon vanilla

Melt the square of chocolate in a mixing bowl over a pan of barely boiling water. Add the butter and mix well. Add the egg and milk and beat for 1 minute. Gradually add the sugar and continue to beat.

Sift the baking soda, baking powder, flour and salt together twice, and then gradually add to the egg-milk mixture. Beat vigorously after each addition. Add the vanilla and beat for 2 minutes longer.

Pour the batter into buttered cupcake tins. Place in a 350° F. oven and bake for ½ hour or until a cake tester comes out clean when inserted in the center of the cupcake. Makes I dozen cupcakes. Frost with your favorite frosting. (See Chapter XIII for 7-minute frosting.)

2-EGG FUDGE LOAF

2 cups light brown sugar
½ cup butter, at room temperature
2 eggs, separated
½ cup dairy sour cream
1 teaspoon baking soda
3 squares semi-sweet <u>ba</u>king chocolate, melted over hot water
½ cup ice cold water
2 cups cake flour

Cream the brown sugar and butter together until thoroughly mixed. Add the egg yolks and beat until the mixture is light and fluffy.

Mix the sour cream and baking soda together and let stand for 2 minutes; then add the sour cream to the sugar mixture and beat again. Add the melted chocolate and beat again.

Alternately add the ice water and the flour, beating after each addition.

Beat the egg whites until they stand in peaks and then gently fold them into the batter, taking care to retain all the air. Pour into a 10- x 5-inch greased loaf pan. Bake in a 375° F. oven for 40 minutes or until a cake tester comes out clean when inserted in the middle of the loaf. Serves 6 generously.

5-EGG FEATHER CAKE

5 eggs, separated
½ teaspoon salt
½ cup ice water
1½ cups sugar
1½ cups cake flour
1 tablespoon lemon juice
1 teaspoon vanilla

Beat the egg yolks and the salt together until they are light and lemon colored, about 1 minute. Add the ice water and beat 1 minute longer.

Sift the sugar and flour together twice and gradually add to the egg yolk mixture, beating after each addition. Add the lemon juice and the vanilla and beat again to mix thoroughly.

Beat the egg whites until they stand in peaks. Gently fold the egg whites into the batter, taking care to retain all the air. Pour into an ungreased 9-inch tubular pan. Place in a 350° F. oven and bake for 50 minutes or until a cake tester comes out clean when inserted in the center portion of the tube. Invert the pan and allow the cake to cool to room temperature before removing. Dust the top and sides of the cake with powdered sugar or frost with your favorite frosting. Serves 8 to 10.